Field Guide to
HORSES

Kindrie Grove

LONE
PINE

THE PUBLISHER: Lone Pine Publishing
206, 10426 – 81 Ave.
Edmonton, AB T6E 1X5
Canada

202A, 1110 Seymour St.
Vancouver, BC V6B 3N3
Canada

1901 Raymond Ave. SW, Suite C
Renton, WA 98055
USA

Website: http://www.lonepinepublishing.com

Canadian Cataloguing in Publication Data

Grove, Kindrie
    Field guide to horses

    Includes index.
    ISBN 1-55105-188-5

1. Horses—Identification. I. Title.
SF285.G76 1998   636.1   C98-910981-X

Editorial Director: Nancy Foulds
Editorial: Nancy Foulds, Rachel Fitz, Erin McCloskey
Production Manager: David Dodge
Design, Layout & Production: Gregory Brown
Cover Design: Michelle Bynoe
Cover Illustrations: Bardigiano, Barb and Thoroughbred by Kindrie Grove
Title Page Illustration: Brumby
Illustrations: Kindrie Grove
Separations & Film: Elite Lithographers Co. Ltd., Edmonton, Alberta
Printing: Quality Color Press, Edmonton, Alberta

The publisher gratefully acknowledges the assistance of the Department
of Canadian Heritage.

Contents

American Walking Pony, p. 24   Assateague/Chincoteague, p. 25   Bardigiano, p. 26

Basuto, p. 27   Canadian Rustic Pony, p. 28   Carpathian Pony, p. 29

Caspian, p. 30   Connemara, p. 31   Dales, p. 32

Dartmoor, p. 33   Exmoor, p. 34   Falabella, p. 36

Fell, p. 37   Gotland, p. 38   Guoxia, p. 39

Hackney Pony, p. 40   Haflinger, p. 41   Highland, p. 42

Icelandic, p. 43

Mérens, p. 44

New Forest, p. 45

Newfoundland Pony, p. 46

Norwegian Fjord, p. 47

Pony of the Americas, p. 48

Sandalwood, p. 49

Shetland, p. 50

Skyros, p. 51

Sorraia, p. 52

Timor, p. 53

Welsh Pony, p. 54

Akhal-Teke, p. 56

Alter-Real, p. 57

American Bashkir Curly, p. 58

American Indian Horse, p. 59

American Quarter Horse, p. 60

American Saddlebred, p. 62

Anglo-Arab, p. 63

Andalusian, p. 64

Arabian, p. 66

Argentine Criollo, p. 68

Banker Horse, p. 69

Barb, p. 70

Brumby, p. 72

Camargue, p. 73

Canadian, p. 74

Cape Horse, p. 76

Carthusian, p. 77

Chickasaw, p. 78

Cleveland Bay, p. 79

Colorado Ranger, p. 80

Don, p. 81

Florida Cracker Horse, p. 82

Frederiksborg, p. 83

Friesian, p. 84

Gelderland, p. 86

Guanzhong, p. 87

Hanoverian, p. 88

Hackney, p. 90

Holstein, p. 91

Kladruber, p. 92

Knabstrup, p. 93

Lipizzan, p. 94

Lusitano, p. 96

Mangalarga Marchador, p. 97

Missouri Fox Trotter, p. 98

Morab, p. 99

Morgan, p. 100

Mustang, p. 102

Namib Desert Horse, p. 103

National Show Horse, p. 104

National Spotted
Saddle Horse, p. 105

Nonius, p. 106

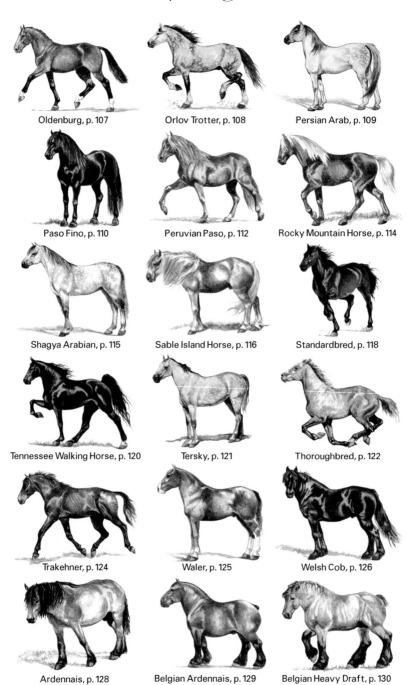

Oldenburg, p. 107

Orlov Trotter, p. 108

Persian Arab, p. 109

Paso Fino, p. 110

Peruvian Paso, p. 112

Rocky Mountain Horse, p. 114

Shagya Arabian, p. 115

Sable Island Horse, p. 116

Standardbred, p. 118

Tennessee Walking Horse, p. 120

Tersky, p. 121

Thoroughbred, p. 122

Trakehner, p. 124

Waler, p. 125

Welsh Cob, p. 126

Ardennais, p. 128

Belgian Ardennais, p. 129

Belgian Heavy Draft, p. 130

Boulonnais, p. 131

Breton, p. 132

Dutch Draft, p. 133

Clydesdale, p. 134

Irish Draft, p. 136

Italian Heavy Draft, p. 137

Jutland, p. 138

Lithuanian Heavy Draft, p. 139

Noriker, p. 140

Percheron, p. 141

Shire, p. 142

Suffolk, p. 144

American Paint, p. 146

Albino, p. 148

Appaloosa, p. 149

Canadian Cutting Horse, p. 150

Canadian Sport Horse, p. 151

Buckskin, p. 152

English Hack, p. 153

English Hunter, p. 154

Palomino, p. 155

Royal Canadian Mounted
Police Horse, p. 156

Pinto, p. 158

Donkey, p. 160

Mule, p. 161

Oneger, p. 162

Tarpan, p. 163

Wild Ass, p. 164

Burchell's Zebra, p. 165

Chapman's Zebra, p. 166

Grant's Zebra, p. 167

Grevy's Zebra, p. 168

Mountain Zebra, p. 169

Przewalski's Horse, p. 170

Introduction

Humans and Horses

'A horse, a horse, my kingdom for a horse!' These famous words, from Shakespeare's *Richard III*, express the depth and significance of the long and illustrious association that humans have had with horses. Modern civilization would not have been possible without the horse. We know that our first cave-dwelling ancestors revered the horse as a source of food and sustenance, but it is unclear when horses ceased to be prey and became the companions of those same ancestors. The paintings of horses and other animals still glitter on the walls and ceilings of caves in the lamplight of today, just as they would have done when the Stone Age artists worked laboriously by torch to depict them.

As the hunter/gatherer existence of the early humans gave way to a more agrarian lifestyle, horses became increasingly valuable. Horses can carry so much more than a human, and as the wheel was developed, they could pull even more. They soon became indispensable. They were present in all the wars, even on the pitched battlefronts. When the saddle was developed, an important tactical advantage became apparent, as a warrior on horseback could be higher than his opponent, and could balance in the saddle's stirrups to wield a weapon.

Horses were important in the recreation of civilization as well. Chariot races, trotting races, mounted galloping races and hunting expeditions are depicted in many cultures around the world, both ancient and recent. Today, equestrian events and shows are practiced worldwide with a great deal of prestige attached to the competitions and the competitors. All these are a testament to the complex and joyful relationship that humans have had with horses.

Evolution of the Horse

Approximately 57 million years ago, during the Eocene era, the Earth would have been all but unrecognizable. The Arctic Circle was covered with lush, semi-tropical vegetation and the continents were much closer together than they are today. There emerged a small creature about a foot (.3 m) tall with four toes on its front feet and three on its back feet, with a rounded back and short slender legs. This creature would later be named Hyracotherium when its fossilized skeleton was discovered by humans. As time passed, other similar fossil remains were found, among them Eohippus, Mesohippus and Miohippus. These were the 'Dawn Horses.'

As the climate of the Earth slowly changed over millions of years and tropical forests and marshes gave way to open woodlands and eventually steppes and expansive grasslands, the first proto-horses evolved. They were much larger than their small, multi-toed ancestors, and they stood on hooves—essentially the middle toe—just as modern horses do. These creatures were named Pliohippus and they walked the Earth some 6 million years ago. Pliohippus is considered to be the direct ancestor to the four horse types that emerged at the end of the Ice Age and from which all breeds of horses sprung.

Although we think of horses as an Old World species, coming from Europe and Asia, they actually evolved on the North American continent. It is thought that groups of 'Dawn Horses' crossed over to Eurasia via the land bridge that existed across the Bering Strait in the Arctic. Pliohippus and eventually *Equus* developed and spread throughout North and South America. Eventually they crossed over to Europe and Asia before the waters of the post-glacial period covered the land bridge. For reasons we may never understand, horses died out in North and South America, while they became ever more diverse in Europe, Asia and Africa. It was not until Spanish explorers landed in South America that the horse began to repopulate the New World.

The Four Early Horse Types

There are four distinctive types of horse that developed in Europe and Asia according to the terrain, climate and habitat that they occupied.

FOREST TYPE

These horses were heavy set and large, adapted to the browsing life of the forests. They had large, round hooves to facilitate walking over ground that was often soft and marshy. Dense coats and long feathers at the fetlocks protected them from a moist climate. They were not built for speed, but then they had nowhere to run in the close forests. The closest relations to the now-extinct Forest Horse are the giant heavy draft horses (pp. 127-144), whose friendly dispositions are well known.

STEPPE TYPE

This type of horse is best represented by Przewalski's Horse (p. 170), which has existed unaltered since the last Ice Age. It had a large head and ears, a stiff, erect mane and a strong, compact body. Its hooves were long and narrow, and it was quick and agile and could easily maneuver over rocks or other rough terrain. This horse type was also unafraid of entering water and was well adapted to life on the steppes.

PLATEAU TYPE

This horse was more lightly built than the Steppe or Forest horses. It had a smaller, more refined head and long, slender legs. It had hooves that were of medium size and width, and it was capable of great speed. It was resistant to drought and hot temperatures and is thought to have given rise to many of the light horse and pony breeds of the world. The Tarpan (p. 163) is the closest relation to this type.

TUNDRA TYPE

This horse type had little influence on the horse and pony breeds of to-day. It roamed northeastern Europe and would have been supremely adapted to that harsh, cold climate. With a coarse head, a wide, long back and short sturdy legs, it was covered in extremely dense, thick fur and had a very long, profuse mane and tail. The native ponies of Siberia evolved from this type. The Guanzhong (p. 87) is representative of the Tundra-type horses, although it is not a descendent.

Anatomy of the Horse

PARTS OF THE HORSE

Different breeds of horse have different 'conformations,' according to the tasks that they perform. Draft horses have a more upright shoulder to better push against the collar of a harness. They have great muscle and bone development and large, wide hooves to help distribute the weight of their immense bulk. Show jumping horses have long legs and well-developed hindquarters to help propel them through the air and over an obstacle. The neck is long and body frame lightweight to keep them agile and fleet. Thoroughbreds are built for speed, and not unlike a greyhound they are long limbed and lean, with small feet that are easy to pick up as they gallop down the track.

All these attributes are part of a horse's conformation, and a horse of a particular breed is judged according to how well its conformation fits with that of its breed.

MARKINGS OF THE HORSE
Face Markings

Star:
  small or large spot of white on forehead.
Stripe:
  thin, white line extending from forehead to tip of nose.
Blaze:
  wide, white strip down middle of face from forehead to nose.
White (bald) face:
  white covering most of the front of the face.
Snip:
  small white strip on tip of nose, often between the nostrils.
White muzzle or lip:
  white marking on lips, chin or muzzle.
Mealy muzzle:
  white or beige muzzle fading into regular coat color.

blaze

star

bald (white) face

snip

white lips (nose)

star & snip

Leg Markings
Sock: white fetlock and leg below the knee.
Stocking: white leg up to the knee and over.
Ermine: black spotting on the white hair of the cornet (lower pastern).

ANATOMY OF THE HORSE

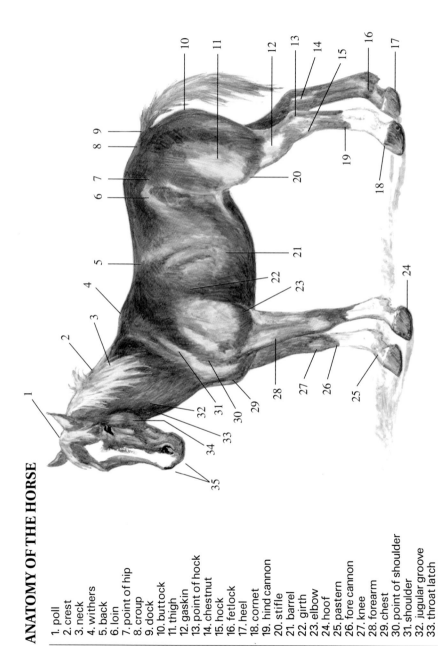

1. poll
2. crest
3. neck
4. withers
5. back
6. loin
7. point of hip
8. croup
9. dock
10. buttock
11. thigh
12. gaskin
13. point of hock
14. chestnut
15. hock
16. fetlock
17. heel
18. cornet
19. hind cannon
20. stifle
21. barrel
22. girth
23. elbow
24. hoof
25. pastern
26. fore cannon
27. knee
28. forearm
29. chest
30. point of shoulder
31. shoulder
32. jugular groove
33. throat latch
34. cheek
35. muzzle

COLORING

The remarkable variety in coloration in the horse species ranges from pure white to jet black and some of the most amazing spotted, speckled and pinto markings. Each horse is very individual and its coat color adds to its uniqueness. Dun and gray coloring are the most dominant colors, but if sire and dam both display a recessive color gene, then the offspring will most likely be the same.

Solid Colors

White or gray: black skin with white hairs; ranges from pure white to dark iron gray. Dapples (light circles on a darker ground) or flea-bitten gray (dark speckles on a lighter ground) are often present.

Black: whole coat color is black, often with white markings on face and/or legs.

Bay: reddish-brown coat varying from very light to very dark with black 'points' (mane, tail, legs and tips of ears).

Brown: coat all over a dark brown, often almost black.

Chestnut or sorrel: reddish-gold coat varying from orange to dark golden, sometimes with light gold mane and tail.

Liver-chestnut: dark brown chestnut, more like a very dark dun than chestnut, with mane and tail the same color.

Dun: sandy-colored coat ranging from dark to light with black points and usually a dorsal stripe down middle of back, and sometimes zebra stripes on the upper legs.

Roan: coat is mostly one solid color interspersed with white hairs; solid color can vary. Blue Roan, Strawberry Roan, Red Roan are named for the overall hue.

Palomino: creamy-golden coat with flaxen or white mane and tail.

Albino: pure white coat with pink skin.

Broken Colors

Spotted: skin color is a mottled pink with either mostly dark hairs interspersed with white spots or speckles, or mostly white hairs with dark spotting. Ground color can range from black to light chestnut. Appaloosas have five spot patterns: snow flake, blanket, leopard, marble and frost.

Pinto: often referred to as 'piebald' (black and white) or 'skewbald' (any other color and white); can be either a white ground with any dark color in large patches ('tobiano') or a dark ground with large white patches ('overo').

SIZES

Horses are measured in hands high (h.h.), from the ground up to the withers. A hand is equivalent to four inches (10 cm), so a horse 14 h.h. would be 52 inches (132 cm) to the withers.

Gaits of the Horse

The term 'gait' refers to the sequence with which each of a horse's four hooves touch the ground. All horses are capable of four main gaits: walk, trot, canter and gallop. Certain breeds of horse, such as the Paso Fino (p. 110) and Tennessee Walker (p. 120), possess a fifth or sixth gait. These extra gaits differ among breeds, but they are invariably very comfortable to ride and are usually inherent in the particular breed. The way that a horse picks its feet up often dictates how comfortable the ride is. A pony's stride tends to be bouncy because it picks its feet up straight and high, whereas a horse tends to bend the leg more at the knee, thus making for a somewhat smoother ride.

Tennessee Walker

Walk: a four-beat gait where each foot is placed on the ground at equal intervals. The opposite fore and hind legs move one after the other. The average speed of the walk is 3 mph (4.8 km/h).

Trot: a two-beat gait in which the opposite fore and hind feet move and land together.

Canter: a three-beat gait where the two hind feet come down one slightly before the other but essentially at the same time. The front feet then touch the ground separately but in the exact same sequence as the hind feet.

Gallop: essentially the same sequence of foot falls as the canter, but a four-beat gait rather than a three. The speed and lengthening of stride in the gallop causes all four feet to touch the ground separately. A horse can maintain a gallop for a short period at a top speed of 43 mph (68.8 km/h).

OTHER GAITS

Pacing: the legs moving forward are both on the same side. Pacing is a very fast and powerful stride.

Amble: a slow version of the pace.

19

Horse Husbandry

BREEDING

A mare carries a foal for 11 months, and the foal is usually born in the spring or summer. A filly will reach sexual maturity at three or four years of age and will come into season, or 'heat,' where she will accept a stallion, about every three weeks during the summer months. A colt will reach breeding maturity at around four years, but in the wild he may not get a chance to breed until he is much older, stronger and more experienced.

A foal will stand on its tiny feet within about a half hour after its birth. Although it can stand, it will take a while to master the movement of those great, long, spindly legs! Mares are very protective of their young and will usually find somewhere quiet and away from other horses to foal. Domestic horses are usually brought inside for protection. A foal's coat is soft and downy, often with a pronounced curl, and its feet, when first born, have a spongy, fibrous growth on the bottom to protect the mother when the foal is in the womb. This growth quickly wears off, and the foal's long legs will straighten and become strong. At six weeks old, a foal will begin to graze grass a little to supplement the mare's milk that will help it grow until it is about six months old. Once it reaches this age, it will usually be weaned either by its dam or its handlers.

A young horse should not be ridden or overworked until it has had a chance to mature physically, usually at about the age of three to four. Horses are fairly long lived and are often still being ridden and worked with into their mid-20s, some even longer! Old horses suffer from the same ailments as humans do when we age. Their eyesight can deteriorate, and they can have sore joints and worn-down teeth. Well-cared for elderly horses can live comfortable lives. It is possible to discover the age of a horse by inspecting its teeth: the longer and more forward slanting a horse's front incisors are, the older it is.

DIET

Horses are herbivores, which means that their diet consists entirely of plant matter. They are grazers, and their teeth are well adapted to clipping off and chewing large quantities of grasses and other coarse sedges. Wild horses munch all spring, summer and fall to fatten up for the winter shortages, and after foraging through the snow and eating dead grass, they are usually quite lean. Most domestic horses have the luxury of being fed what they need during the times that they cannot graze. Horses only have one stomach, unlike other ungulates such as deer or bison, and as a result they don't have to chew their cud.

A stabled horse generally needs to be fed a sufficient quantity of hay, with a large bucket of water to slake thirst. Often a supplement of grain or some mineral-rich feed is added to the diet, especially for a mare in foal. Horses also require a salt lick, which comes in the form of a big block for domestic use.

CARE AND EXERCISE

There is a wonderful saying that has a ring of truth to it: 'Horses make the young older and the old younger.' Indeed, much joy has been shared at the wonder of horses.

Horses are large, intelligent and sensitive animals that require a lot of attention, especially if they are stabled indoors away from other horses. In a stable, a horse can very easily become bored and irritable. They need lots of exercise and fresh air as well as mental stimulation. They are carefree creatures that enjoy play with other horses and people.

Grooming and working with a horse on the ground goes a long way towards promoting trust and a meaningful partnership while in or under the saddle. Basic grooming tools include brushes, rubbing gloves, a shedding tool, a hoof pick and a cloth or anything else that lends itself to the task.

English tack

Western tack

TACK

There are two main styles of riding in Europe and North America: English Pleasure and Western Pleasure. Both riding styles have their own type of gear, or 'tack.' Within each type are also many differences. For example, dressage requires a certain type of English saddle, as does jumping or hunting, and in Western there are differences between roping saddles, barrel racing saddles and basic stock saddles. Head gear also varies depending on use or the disposition or training level of the horse wearing the bridle.

Horse Psychology

Horses are herd animals and are happiest when they are surrounded by their own kind. Each horse has a distinct and individual personality: some are quirky and lighthearted, others are shy and tentative, and others are friendly and forward. Observing horses together shows a complex and effective social system. There are rules that they follow and a very concise language made up of subtle body movements and gestures, much of which we completely miss. Horses are also animals of instinct, and the flight response in them is very strong. They are more likely to flee from a situation they don't understand than to let their curiosity get in the way. But if their level of trust is high and they are comfortable in their relationship with humans, it is easy enough for them to overcome their fear and let curiosity lead the way.

In the wild and where domestication permits it, horses will roam in family groups of up to 25 members, consisting of a dominant mare, subordinate mares, juveniles and a single stallion. It is actually the head mare who makes the day-to-day decisions for the herd, and the others take their lead from her, but they will always look to the stallion for protection. When a colt reaches maturity, he will leave the group to wander on his own or join a bachelor group where he will prepare for the day when he is able to find or steal mares of his own.

Horses in Mythology and Art

We need only look to the world's infinite mythologies and art to understand how important the horse has been to the human race—from the great Trojan Horse filled with Greek soldiers waiting for their unsuspecting foe to bring the horse within their walls, to the mythical unicorn of the Middle Ages that could only be caught by a virgin. Such myths and legends tell of our close connection to the horse. They play a strong role in the ancient art of Europe and Asia. A multitude of statues and paintings depict horses in all their glory.

In times of war and in times of peace, for farming and traveling, for competition and sport, people have historically always had the horse at their side. It is, I think, a situation not likely to change soon!

Ponies

American Walking Pony

Developed by crossing the Tennessee Walking Horse and the Welsh Pony, the American Walking Pony is a fairly recent breed in the United States. It combines the inherent walking gaits of the Tennessee Walker and the refined look and great jumping ability of the Welsh Pony. An extremely versatile pony, it has two unique gaits—the 'pleasure walk' and the 'merry walk'—which are very comfortable to sit.

Origin: United States of America
Average Height: Up to 14 h.h.
Aptitudes: Riding

The American Walking Pony has a fine, chiseled head with large, wide-set eyes, small, mobile ears and a small muzzle; neck arched and long, set high on sloped shoulders; back short and straight, with a deep girth; croup moderately sloped, and tail set at medium height; legs straight, with hocks on hind legs sometimes turned in; hooves small; color usually solid.

Assateague/Chincoteague

The Assateague and Chincoteague ponies live on Assateague Island, off the coast of Maryland and Virginia. They are divided by a fence that represents the border between the two states, but they are essentially the same pony. Stories about how the ponies got to the island are plentiful, ranging from Spanish colonial horses surviving a shipwreck and swimming ashore, to horses left on the island by pirates. Most likely they are the descendants of horses released on the island by colonists. Every July, for the famous 'Pony Penning' carnival, the ponies are rounded up to swim the Chincoteague River. They stay one night at the carnival grounds, and then are released to swim back to the island. The ponies are quite a well-known attraction and are very accustomed to people.

The Assateague and Chincoteague ponies roam in small bands, led by a herd stallion who keeps his group together and defends it from other stallions. Left to develop on their own, the ponies have become hardy, tough and well adapted to roaming the island and grazing the salty marsh grasses. The head is small, with wide-set eyes; muzzle and ears small; withers prominent; tail set low; legs strong and slim; hooves hard; color varies, pintos common.

Origin: United States of America
Average Height: 12 to 14 h.h.
Aptitudes: Wild pony, but sometimes trained to ride

Bardigiano

Bearing a strong resemblance to the Dales pony of England and the Mérens pony of France, the Bardigiano is also a pony of ancient origins. It is thought to have come to Italy with the Germanic warriors who traveled to the Apennine Mountains, where the pony found a permanent home. The Bardigiano is named after the village of Bardi, where a Medieval castle stands. These robust ponies became very homogeneous in their isolated mountain pastures, well adapted to the rigors of the steep terrain. They were used to produce mules for the Italian army during World Wars I and II. The breed declined after that and it was only recently that attempts were made to reintroduce it.

Origin: Italy
Average Height: 13.2 to 14.1 h.h.
Aptitudes: Riding and light draft

Bardigianos have fine heads with a slightly dished profile and large eyes; muzzle is wide, with a jutting upper lip; neck medium length and thickly crested, set into sloped shoulders and a very wide, deep chest; back medium length; croup well developed and rounded; legs strong and short, with short pasterns and large, very hard hooves; mane and tail long and profuse; color bay, very dark to light, with a small white star sometimes seen on the forehead, and white fetlocks.

Basuto

Cape Horses began to arrive in Basutoland (now Lesotho) during the early 19th century. They were bought from European traders and were raided from other tribes who had likely stolen them from Dutch settlers living near the South African border. The Basuto ponies, unlike their predecessor the Cape Horse, became smaller owing to the extremely harsh, high-altitude climate of Lesotho. The Basuto strongly resembles the Mongolian horse, which is among the first Oriental breeds brought to the Cape area of South Africa. The main breeds from which the Cape Horse developed were the Arab, the Barb and the Thoroughbred, all of which were passed on in the development of the hardy Basuto pony.

Considered, in Lesotho, to be a small horse and not a pony, the Basuto has a medium-sized head, prominent jaw and straight profile; neck long and thin, set into pronounced withers; back long; shoulders fairly upright; croup sloped; tail set low; legs clean and slim; feet very hard; color usually chestnut, gray, brown and bay.

Origin: Lesotho
Average Height: 14 to 14.2 h.h.
Aptitudes: Riding and light draft

Canadian Rustic Pony

A rare sight, the Canadian Rustic Pony originated in the provinces of Manitoba and Saskatchewan, and is slowly gaining in popularity throughout the rest of Canada and the United States. A quarter of this stout pony's makeup comes from the Tarpan, an Ice Age horse, which gives the Canadian Rustic its distinctive features: short stand-up mane, dark dorsal stripe down the back and zebra striping on its legs! Arab and Welsh Mountain Pony contribute to the rest of the Canadian Rustic Pony's background.

Origin: Canada
Average Height: 12.2 to 13.2 h.h.
Aptitudes: Riding

The Canadian Rustic is an amazingly hardy and versatile pony. Owners of this unique breed testify to its character most enthusiastically and praise its many abilities. This pony has a smallish head, with a dished or straight profile; muzzle small; eyes large and wide set; neck thick, with a short, standing mane; back short and straight, with a dark dorsal stripe; legs strong and usually dark, with zebra striping; hooves strong and hard; color can be many solid shades of brown or gray.

Carpathian Pony

The Carpathian Pony, also known as the Hucul, originated in the Carpathian Mountains of Romania and Poland. It is thought to be descended from the crossing of the wild Tarpan and the Mongolian horse. Three different types of Carpathians have emerged, a saddle, a pack and a draft, with the pack type being the most popular. Carpathians are well known for their hardiness and surefootedness. They rarely suffer from ailments of any kind and make gentle companions.

Carpathians have short heads and large eyes; neck and back strong and muscular; croup rounded but short; legs dense and strong; hooves small and very hard; zebra striping on legs and dorsal stripe down back commonly seen; color bay and dun most commonly, but others seen as well.

Origin: Carpathian Mountains of Poland, Romania
Average Height: 12.2 to 14 h.h.
Aptitudes: Riding and light draft

Caspian

In 1965 the Caspian was encountered around the Caspian Sea roaming and laboring for the local people. So distinctive in its appearance was this little horse that it raised many questions. It has since been theorized that the Caspian is the ancient miniature horse used by the Mesopotamians for centuries, and previously thought to be extinct. If the conjecture is true and a direct line can be traced from the Caspian to those horses of old, it could mean that it is the ancestor to all of today's hotblood horses!

Origin: Persia (Iran)

Average Height: 9.2 to 11.2 h.h.

Aptitudes: Riding, jumping and light draft

Caspians differ from modern horses in their skeletal structure, most apparently by the bulging or domed forehead and the narrow oval-shaped hooves. They are small horses, not ponies, and show no pony characteristics. With great athletic abilities in both jumping and harness, the little Caspian is making a strong comeback from the brink of extinction.

They are like the Arab with a prominent, domed forehead and large, expressive eyes, tiny ears, small muzzle and a lovely arched neck; shoulders sloped; back straight; croup quite flat; tail set high; legs slim and strong; hooves oval and very hard; color usually brown, bay, gray and chestnut.

Connemara

L ike so many other ponies of the British Isles, the Connemara is likely a descendant of the early Celtic ponies. The Connemara is the only pony native to Ireland. It derives its name from the westernmost county of Connemara, where it developed hardiness and intelligence roaming the rugged, exposed coastline. Andalusian and Clydesdale blood were introduced to the Connemara over time, and recently Arab has been used to add refinement.

Connemara ponies are well known for their jumping ability, and they are large enough to make good mounts for adults. They have a handsome head with a straight profile, small pricked ears and

Origin: Ireland
Average Height: 13 to 14.2 h.h.
Aptitudes: Riding and light draft

large eyes; neck fairly long and arched, with some cresting; shoulders very sloped and chest deep; withers prominent but well integrated into back and neck; back longish and straight; hindquarters round and strong; legs clean and strong, with well-defined joints; hooves hard; mane and tail long and thick; color, though once almost primarily dun, now includes gray, black, brown, bay and sometimes roan and chestnut.

Dales

The Dales pony is a native of the dales of northern England, and is thought to descend from the early Celtic horses. Outcrossing to Welsh Cob, Scotch Galloway (now extinct) and Norfolk Trotter made the Dales an excellent farm pony and a great trotter. It was used in the local lead mines and acquired a reputation for carrying extraordinarily heavy loads. During World War II, little attention was paid to this breed; often they were killed for food. As a result, these stout ponies were almost lost, but because of their superior abilities on the hill farms where larger horses couldn't maneuver as well, they began to make a comeback.

Origin: England
Average Height: 13.2 to 14.2 h.h.
Aptitudes: Riding, light draft and driving

Dales have a small head with a straight profile, wide-set eyes and small ears; neck short, thick and muscular, set on sloped shoulders; chest broad, with a short back; croup sloped; hindquarters very muscular; legs strong with a good deal of bone; mane and tail long and thick; lower legs feathered; color predominantly black, but dark brown and gray are seen, and white markings are rare.

Dartmoor

Much like the Exmoor, the Dartmoor is an old breed that has inhabited the Dartmoor area of Devonshire in England for thousands of years. It is not as pure in its ancient lineage as the Exmoor, having been outcrossed with Arab and Welsh Cob, but it retains the trait of supreme hardiness in harsh conditions. It is a surefooted little pony with a natural jumping ability, and makes an excellent children's mount.

Bred mainly as a wild pony, the Dartmoor has a small head with wide-set eyes and small, pointed ears; neck thick and of medium length; body compact; shoulder well sloped; back short; hindquarters well developed; tail set fairly high; legs tough and dense; hooves hard; mane and tail very thick and long; color predominantly bay, black and brown, with gray seen as well, and white markings are uncommon.

Origin: England
Average Height: 11.2 to 12.2 h.h.
Aptitudes: Riding

Exmoor

The oldest known native breed of Great Britain, the Exmoor is famous for its hardiness. It is surefooted, nimble and well adapted to life on the wild moorlands of southwestern England. It is thought that the Exmoor is a direct descendant from Ice Age horses that came from North America across Europe to Great Britain before it was an island, during the last Ice Age. An amazing link has been found that connects the Exmoor to fossil records of horses found in North America. The jaw bones of the Exmoor are surprisingly similar to those of the fossil records, including the beginning of a seventh molar tooth, a characteristic found in no other breed of pony or horse alive today! The Exmoor has undoubtedly inherited its dense, wiry, almost waterproof coat, distinctive coloring and ability to survive almost any weather from its Ice Age ancestors.

Origin: Great Britain
Average Height: 11.1 to 12.3 h.h.
Aptitudes: Riding and light draft

Exmoor ponies still run free on the moors. Although the few foundation herds left are owned by people, they are left largely to themselves to continue on as they have done for centuries. Exmoors have also been instrumental in founding many other horse breeds, passing on their tremendously hardy nature. They are fiercely independent and self-sufficient.

Exmoors have a short, thick head with a straight profile; eyes large and wide set; ears short and wide set; neck fairly thick and short; shoulders sloped; chest broad; legs strong; feet small and hard; mane thick; tail distinctively 'ice,' with hairs growing out in fan shape; color usually bay brown or dun, with distinctive 'mealy' or creamy areas around the eyes, muzzle, underbelly and inside of thighs.

Falabella

A t about 30 inches (75 cm) high, the Falabella horses are the smallest horses in the world! As you can imagine, these tiny horses are not suitable for riding but can often be seen in harness, pulling miniature wagons and carts that seat two people. They are also much sought-after as a pet. Despite their size, Falabellas are surprisingly strong and hardy, and they can live to an incredible age of 45 years. Named for the family that developed this miniature, Falabella horses have been bred from a combination of many breeds, including Shetland, Criollo and small English Thoroughbred. Their diminutive size makes these miniature horses very easy to pick out in a field; the size was achieved by cross-breeding only the smallest horses.

Origin: Argentina
Average Height: 6.1 to 7 h.h.
Aptitudes: Light harness

Falabellas are intelligent, gentle little horses that differ from large horses only in size. Mane and tail vary in length and thickness; legs fine boned; hooves small and oval; color varies.

Fell

Smaller than its native cousin the Dales pony, the Fell pony evolved separately from the Dales after the end of the 19th century. As the Dales began to gain size, the Fells retained their small size and compact build. Today they are known for their harness ability and their versatility as a riding pony. When the Romans landed on the British Isles, they brought over the ancient Friesian from Friesland to aid in the building of many works. As a result, the native mountain ponies were influenced by these great black horses, including the Fell, Dales and even the modern day Shire (known also as the Old English Black). During the Industrial Revolution the Fell pony was almost lost, but with the generous support of King George V and Beatrix Potter, no less, the Fell pony was revived early in the 20th century.

The Fell has a small, fine head, prominent, bright eyes and small ears; neck strong and slightly crested; back long and straight; shoulders well sloped; tail set low; hindquarters square and muscular;

Origin: England
Average Height: 13 to 14 h.h.
Aptitudes: Riding, driving and light draft

legs strong and muscular, with large joints; feet hard and round; mane and tail long and profuse, with feathering on the lower legs; color usually black, brown, bay and gray, with occasional white markings.

Gotland

The Gotland pony has endured on the Island of Gotland since the Stone Age. It is thought to be a descendant of the Tarpan and, except for an introduction of Oriental blood at some point, it has remained unchanged. Much like the Exmoor of Great Britain, this stout pony is hardy and tough, owing many of its traits to prehistoric ancestors.

Representations of chariot horses remarkably similar to Gotlands can be seen in the ancient civilization of the Goths. It is believed that the Gotland pony expanded into northern Europe with the Goths, and as a result, many breeds in northern Europe claim some of their origins from the ancient Gotland.

Origin: Sweden
Average Height: 11.2 to 13 h.h.
Aptitudes: Riding and light draft

Gotlands are bred today throughout Sweden and a few places in the United States. They are noted for their great trotting ability, but are also good jumpers and children's ponies. They are light and refined; head small and straight in profile; eyes wide set; ears small; neck short; back long; tail set low; legs strong and slim; hooves hard; color usually dun, with a dorsal stripe, but can be other solid colors.

Guoxia

A native of China, the tiny Guoxia is an ancient breed. There is debate about whether it is a tiny pony or a miniature horse, since it seems to have more horse traits than pony. Bronze statues of Guoxia horses discovered in Guanxi Province date back 2000 years, indeed a testament to this breed's great antiquity! Guoxia means 'under fruit tree horse,' which is an apt name considering its small size. Today the extremely hardy and agile Guoxias are used mainly as children's pets.

Guoxias have short heads with straight profiles; ears small; eyes large; muzzle small; neck short and thick; shoulders sloped; back and croup straight with low withers; hindquarters gently sloped and round; legs fine and straight, with strong joints; hooves small, narrow and hard; color usually bay, gray and roan.

Origin: Southwest China
Average Height: 9 to 10 h.h.
Aptitudes: Riding and light draft

Hackney Pony

The word 'hack' or 'hackney' was historically used to describe 'a horse let out for common hire,' or 'a horse worn out in service.' It is ironic that a breed of horse highly esteemed for its flashy, high-stepping, dramatic elegance should be described as such. The Hackney Pony breed was established in 1872 in England. It stemmed from the Hackney horse, which is a larger version of the pony, and a combination of Welsh and Fell ponies. Hackney ponies are bred mainly for the show ring in Europe and North America today, where they can be seen in harness pulling light carriages. They are indeed an impressive sight as they pass by all but flying over the ground, head and tail held high and hooves beating the quick rhythm of their high, graceful step.

Origin: England
Average Height: 12.1 to 14.1 h.h.
Aptitudes: Harness and riding

Hackney ponies have refined heads with large eyes; ears small and pricked; neck arched and muscular, with head carriage high; back short; croup gently sloped; legs fine but very strong; feet hard; tail carried high; color may be brown, black, gray, roan, or bay, with white markings.

Haflinger

Originating in the mountains of Austria, the Haflinger is a unique and hardy pony. Haflinger ancestry consists of the local robust horses of the Austrian mountains and Arabian blood introduced during the 1800s. Isolation from other horses, owing to the harsh, rocky terrain of its mountainous habitat, has created a horse that breeds always to type. In fact, it is impossible to find a Haflinger that does not have the characteristic golden coat and white mane and tail!

Haflingers are well known for their astounding strength and longevity. Some owners claim that their horses have been working for them at the age of 40! They have a lovely, refined head quite reminiscent of the Arab, with large eyes and small ears; neck muscular and arched; body very robust, with sloped shoulders and strong sloped hindquarters; legs well muscled, with plenty of dense bone; tail set low; hooves hard; mane and tail white, and usually a white face or blaze, and stockings.

Origin: Austria
Average Height: 13 to 14.2 h.h.
Aptitudes: Riding and light draft

Highland

The Highland is another pony of great antiquity. It roamed the Scottish Highlands before even the last Ice Age, and like so many other ponies that have not greatly changed from their prehistoric ancestors, the Highland is extremely hardy and tough. Highland ponies were often used instead of larger horses by the Scots during the Middle Ages because of their surefootedness and strength. Even Robert the Bruce, the famed 14th-century king of Scotland, is reputed to have ridden a Highland pony!

There are two types of Highland pony found in Scotland: the mainland type known as the Garron, and the Western Isles type, which is smaller than the former and thought to be a closer representation of the Ice Age Highland. These stout, agile ponies are used today primarily as hunting mounts to carry deer down from the hilly hunting grounds, and as trekking ponies.

Origin: Scotland
Average Height: 12.2 to 14.2 h.h.
Aptitudes: Riding, light draft and pack

They have short heads with wide-set eyes and small ears, and open, wide nostrils; neck strong and medium length, set into powerful, well-sloped shoulders; chest broad; girth deep; back short, with round, gently sloping croup and strong hindquarters; legs short and very sound, with feathered fetlocks; hooves hard and wide; color often a primitive dun, with a dorsal stripe and zebra stripes on the legs, and gray, chestnut, black and bay.

Icelandic

The only national horse breed of Iceland, the Icelandic horse, though small in stature, is considered by Icelanders to be a horse and not a pony. Icelandics are bred for adult riders and are indeed a lot of horse to be sitting upon. These sturdy little horses are one of the oldest breeds of horses in the world. Icelandic horses have remained isolated from the rest of the world's horse breeds for 1000 years, and as a result they are exceedingly pure of blood, although, owing to isolation, they have lost much of their natural defenses against diseases. As a result, Iceland has very strict regulations regarding the export and import of horses and horse gear. Because of their isolation, Icelandic horses have retained the five gaits for which they are famous. The gait they are so well known for is called the 'tolt,' which is a fast ambling gait that is very comfortable and covers a great amount of ground. It is possible to find Icelandic horses in many countries throughout the world.

Icelandic horses are very hardy, tough and extremely long lived. Records show that one horse lived to the amazing age of 56! They have a large head with a straight profile and a thick neck; shoulder long and sloped; back straight; croup sloped; hindquarters muscular; legs strong and dense; hooves very hard; mane and tail very thick; color varies.

Origin: Iceland
Average Height: 12 to 13.1 h.h.
Aptitudes: Riding

Mérens

Bearing a strong resemblance to the Dale and Fell ponies of the British Isles and the ancient black Friesian, the Mérens has been relatively isolated throughout its development. It has roamed the area of the Ariegeois Mountains of southern France since the Ice Age. These stout ponies live in semi-wild herds and have marked Oriental features. They are extremely surefooted and strong, able to carry adults over rough ground.

Origin: France
Average Height: 13 to 14 h.h.
Aptitudes: Riding and light draft

Their heads are well shaped, with a wide, flat forehead, large eyes and wide nostrils; neck short and thick, set into prominent withers and well-sloped shoulders; back long and strong; croup round, with strong hindquarters; legs shortish and sturdy, with broad knees and hocks; hooves hard; mane and tail long and full; fetlocks feathered; color always black, with rarely white markings of any kind.

New Forest

Like so many other native British ponies, the New Forest is hardy and tough, making it an excellent mount for riding, jumping and other equestrian events. It originated in the area that shares its name, the New Forest on the English coast. It seems that there have been horses in that area since the Celts worshipped Epona, the goddess of horse breeders. The New Forest has historically been the hunting grounds for the kings of England, and the sturdy ponies roamed there for centuries before becoming predominantly privately owned.

New Forest ponies have pony-type heads on a shortish neck and well-sloped shoulders; back short; hindquarters strong and sloped; girth deep; legs strong, with joints well defined; hooves hard; color solid.

Origin: England
Average Height: 12 to 14.2 h.h.
Aptitudes: Riding and light draft

Newfoundland Pony

If you ever find yourself on the Island of Newfoundland, you might see a little-known pony that is found there almost exclusively. The New-foundland Pony has been there for centuries, brought over from England by the first settlers. These stout ponies have been vital to the rural life of this easternmost province. They were essential to the planting and reaping of the harvest, pulling sledges in the winter snow and for general farm labor. Throughout the summer, the ponies were turned loose to wander and breed without hindrance. As a result, they developed naturally, with the fittest surviving to pass on their tried and tested genes. Interest in Newfoundland Ponies has recently gained momentum.

Origin: Canada
Average Height: 12 to 14 h.h.
Aptitudes: Riding and light draft

They have small heads, large eyes and pricked ears with a great deal of fur in them; neck strong and thick; body well built and sturdy; mane and tail thick, with mane falling on both sides of the neck in winter; color mainly brown, black, bay and roan.

Norwegian Fjord

The ancient horse of the Vikings, the Norwegian Fjord has been around for centuries. The Vikings used this stout, strong little pony for war mounts and farm labor, and their invasions of many parts of Europe saw the little Fjords expand their territory as well. It is thought that many of the draft breeds that developed over time owe some of their parentage to the Norwegian Fjord.

Very distinctive in appearance, the Fjord is always dun in color with a dark dorsal stripe down its back and zebra striping on its legs. Its mane usually stands up straight, with the black of the dorsal stripe extending up through the middle of it. Fjords are very popular around the world and are bred in many countries, including Canada and the United States. Owing to their unique physical appearance, Fjords are easily recognizable.

Origin: Norway
Average Height: 13 to 14.2 h.h.
Aptitudes: Riding and light draft

A very stout pony, Norwegian Fjords have a medium-sized head with very wide-set eyes and small ears; profile slightly concave; jaw pronounced; neck short and muscular, set on low withers and very sloped shoulders; back short; croup sloped, with well-developed hindquarters; legs short and strong, with large joints; hooves hard.

47

Pony of the Americas

The Pony of the Americas was established about 20 years ago by crossing Shetland ponies with Appaloosas. The result was a much-needed large pony suitable for children and adults. Today the Pony of the Americas Club is one of the most active and popular breed associations geared toward young people in the world. If you happen to see a spotted pony in a field, chances are it is a Pony of the Americas.

Origin: United States of America
Average Height: 11.2 to 14 h.h.
Aptitudes: Riding

Pony of the Americas are very refined (not heavy boned), more like small horses than ponies, and they are admired for their immense versatility. They have a small Arab-type head with large eyes, usually showing the whites, and medium-sized ears; neck slightly arched and long, set on sloped shoulders; back short and straight, with rounded croup; legs straight and solid; hooves broad, often striped; color always spotted, showing all the Appaloosa colors.

Sandalwood

This native pony of the Islands of Sumba and Sumbawa is well loved throughout Indonesia. Named after the principal export of Indonesia, the Sandalwood is a pony with remarkable powers of endurance. It is raced bareback throughout Indonesia and it is even said that Sandalwood ponies rarely sweat! It is perhaps the most refined of all of Indonesia's pony breeds, because of the large amount of Arabian blood that it carries. It is often bred to Thoroughbreds to produce a quality horse for racing throughout Southeast Asia.

Sandalwoods have refined Arab-type heads with large, expressive eyes; neck long and well shaped, set into a deep chest and sloped shoulders; back straight and long, with fairly level croup; legs fine and strong; hooves hard; lower leg free of hair and coat very fine; color varies, most common colors are seen.

Origin: Indonesia
Average Height: 12.1 to 13.1 h.h.
Aptitudes: Riding, racing and light draft

Shetland

Often known as 'Scotland's Little Giant,' the Shetland is the smallest pony breed. Its origins are believed to stem from the ponies of Scandinavia, Ireland and Wales, which must have traveled to the Shetland Islands off the coast of Scotland before the lands separated around 8000 BC. They were subsequently brought to Scotland by the Celts. Shetlands were used extensively in the coal mines of Europe, where it was difficult for even a small child to stand up straight.

Origin: Scotland
Average: No taller than 10.2 h.h.
Aptitudes: Riding and light draft

Evolving in the harsh weather of Scotland and Scandinavia, Shetlands are extremely hardy and long lived. They are also very strong, able to carry half of their body weight. Today Shetlands make excellent children's mounts, as long as the ponies are not spoiled. The American Shetland is a common sight in both the United States and Canada. Shetlands are stout and lively. The head is small with large, kind eyes and small ears and muzzle; neck short and thick; back short and very strong, with deep girth; legs short and very sound; hooves small and hard; mane and tail thick and very long; winter coat also very long and dense; color varies, including piebald and skewbald.

Skyros

Developed on the Island of Skyros off the coast of Greece, the Skyros pony is often described as a small horse. It is very similar to the Caspian in appearance and is thought to descend from the Tarpan-type horse. It is the smallest pony of Greece and has lived on the rocky, mountainous Skyros for centuries. As a result, it is extremely hardy, thrifty and ideally suited to the island's environment. On Skyros it was often used for farm labor during the summer and then turned loose for the winter to roam the island in semi-wild herds. It is popular on the Greek mainland as a children's mount.

The Skyros is very small with a delicate body structure and an attractive head; forehead wide, with small ears and large eyes; neck slim and medium length, set into upright shoulders; back straight and

Origin: Greece
Average Height: 9.1 to 11 h.h.
Aptitudes: Riding and light draft

hip short, with a sloped croup; legs fine boned and long, with a tendency for the hinds to be cow-hocked; hooves so hard that this small pony rarely needs to be shod; mane and tail long and full; color usually bay, with brown, gray and dun seen as well.

Sorraia

This ancient breed of horse is thought to be very closely related to the Tarpan and Przewalski's horses. It exhibits many 'primitive' character-istics and is likely to have changed very little since prehistoric times. It is extremely hardy and able to withstand the harshest climates with poor forage. Sorraias are thought also to have contributed greatly to the Andalusian and, as a result, indirectly to many breeds throughout Europe. Sorraias were among the first horses to be brought to South America by the Spanish, most likely to be used as pack animals, which could explain why there are many horses in North America today bearing 'primitive' dun characteristics.

Origin: Spain, Portugal
Average Height: 12.2 to 13.2 h.h.
Aptitudes: Riding and pack animal

Sorraias have large heads with straight or convex profiles, high-set eyes and long, black-tipped ears; neck slender and long, set into prominent withers and upright shoulders; back straight and croup sloped, with a low tail set; hindquarters tend to be underdeveloped; legs rather long; hooves dark and extremely hard; color usually dun with black points; mane and tail black, often with dun high-lights; legs and shoulder zebra striped and dorsal stripe common.

Timor

This immensely strong little pony is the smallest of the Indonesian ponies. It was most likely introduced to the Island of Timor by the Portuguese, who had a colony there. The people of Indonesia have prized the little Timor pony for its powers of endurance and its common-sense personality. They use it for everything from working with cattle to farm labor. It was also one of the first horse breeds taken to Australia, where it played an important role in the development of the Waler horse.

These ponies have small heads, with a straight profile and short ears; neck short and muscular; withers pronounced, with a fairly upright shoulder; back short and straight, with a sloped croup and low tail set; legs short and very strong, with dense bone; hooves small and very hard; color usually bay, black or brown, but any color variation can be seen.

Origin: Indonesia
Average Height: 10 to 12 h.h.
Aptitudes: Riding and light draft

Welsh Pony

There are three different types of Welsh Pony: the Welsh Mountain Pony, the Welsh Pony and the Welsh Pony of Cob Type. The Welsh Mountain Pony is the smallest of the three. It is also the oldest, thought to descend from the ancient Celtic ponies. It evolved in the hills of Wales before the Romans inhabited that area. The Welsh Pony is very much like the Welsh Mountain Pony, only larger, having been outcrossed with Hackney and a small Thoroughbred stallion named Merlin. The Welsh Pony of Cob Type is of a much heavier build than the others. As a result, it makes an excellent trekking mount and a great all-round riding and driving pony. The Cob Type was developed with the help of the Andalusian, Welsh Cob and Welsh Mountain Pony.

Origin: Wales
Average Height: Welsh Mountain Pony no larger than 12.2 h.h.; Welsh Pony 12.2 to 13.2 h.h.; Welsh Pony of Cob Type no larger than 13.2 h.h.
Aptitudes: Riding, driving and light draft

All three ponies are very similar, except that the Cob Type is generally more stocky and robust than its lighter and smaller cousins, and there are some color variations. They have small heads with large, wide-set eyes and small, pricked ears; profile either slightly dished or straight; neck arched and well set on sloped shoulders; back short, with a slightly sloping croup; girth deep; legs strong, with short cannon bones; hooves hard and round; color solid. Welsh and Welsh Cob Type Ponies are also solid in color, although piebald and skewbald are also seen.

Light
Horses

Akhal-Teke

Direct descendants of the now-extinct horse the Sythians of Persia so cherished—the Turkmenian—can be seen today in the ancient breed of the Akhal-Teke. They also bear a striking resemblance to the Arabian horse, which is also a descendent of the Turkmenian. The Akhal-Teke has remained relatively unchanged up to the present, and efforts are being made today to keep it that way.

Origin: Turkmenistan
Average Height: 14.2 to 16 h.h.
Aptitudes: Riding and racing

Akhal-Tekes have exceptional endurance. They were desert-bred and raised, and have less need of water and food than other horses. An amazing cross-country trek was undertaken by people riding these horses from Ashkhabad to Moscow in 1935. The trek was 1800 miles (2898 km) long, 300 miles (483 km) of which was over desert with no water!

Extremely light and narrow of build, the Akhal-Teke has an angular appearance; head fine, straight and wedge-shaped; mane and tail thin; neck long and slender; withers prominent; back long; croup straight; chest narrow; legs slender and long but very hard; hooves large and very hard; color commonly a distinctive metallic dun, but black, gray and bay can occur, and white markings on legs and heads are prevalent.

Alter-Real

The word 'real' means royal in Portuguese, and the horses bred at the Stud of the Royal Family of Portugal during the 1700s were aptly named Alter-Real. They stemmed from 300 Andalusian mares imported from Spain by the Royal Family. When Napoleon invaded, there was a diluting of the Alter-Real with Arab, Thoroughbred, Hanoverian and Norman. The resulting horse was greatly changed from its original form, and it was not until Andalusian blood was once again introduced that the Alter-Real began to approach its former greatness.

Owing to the large amount of Andalusian blood in the Alter-Real, the two horses resemble one another quite a bit. Alter-Reals have a reputation for being highly strung, but they can make tremendous saddle horses. They have medium-sized

Origin: Portugal
Average Height: 15 to 16 h.h.
Aptitudes: Riding

heads, with large, wide-set eyes; neck crested and set on very sloped shoulders; back short and compact, with powerful, rounded hindquarters; legs fine, with hard bone and long pasterns that give the horses a high-stepping action; color almost always bay.

57

American Bashkir Curly

I t is difficult to say how a few horses with tight curly hair all over their bodies were found in the high country of central Nevada. There are many speculations about how they got there, but none seems to explain the mystery. Nevertheless, two men riding through the mountains of central Nevada in 1898 came across three curly haired horses. This discovery led to the development of the American Bashkir Curly.

Origin: United States of America
Average Height: 14.3 to 15 h.h.
Aptitudes: Riding horse of much versatility

These horses have curly coats with feathers on their feet, and even the hair in their ears is curly. They have the unique trait of frequently shedding out both mane and tail hair during the summer. They are hardy horses of medium size; head smallish, with eyes wide set; back short and rump round; legs straight, with very round; hooves hard; color varies, solid or broken.

American Indian Horse

The history of North American Native culture is intertwined with the horse. When Columbus and the Spaniards came to South America beginning in the late 15th century, they brought their Andalusian horses. Over the years, the descendants of those Spanish horses spread throughout North America and became an integral part of the Native tribes. With the horse came more mobility, greater speed for hunting and an easier mode of transportation. The American Indian Horse is a breed that came about through the need to preserve the blood lines of this horse. With an immensely colorful past, it is a horse that has seen all of North and South American history since Columbus landed in 1492!

There are many different classifications for the American Indian Horse depending on their type and size. The classification varies also according to modern breeds and how much their pedigree includes the Spanish blood. In short, they can be any horse that can be traced to a specific Native tribe, and they can be any color, broken or solid.

Origin: United States of America
Average Height: 13 to 15 h.h
Aptitudes: Riding

American Quarter Horse

The American Quarter Horse is one of the best-known horses in North America. Originally it was bred for racing, its ancestry being from a cross between the Spanish horses and those imported by the colonists. In the early 1600s, there were few racetracks of the type that we have today. The races run by these horses were often quite short, often just the main street of town. A quarter mile (.4 km) was the distance usually raced, and so the Quarter Horse was aptly named after the quarter mile that it ran. By the time that Thoroughbreds began arriving in North America, Quarter Horses were already well established. When Thoroughbreds were pitted against Quarter Horses for these short races, the smaller, stockier Quarter Horses, with their quicksilver starts, invariably won, much to the great chagrin of the Thoroughbred owners. Over longer distances, though, the Thoroughbred could outlast the Quarter Horse.

Origin: United States of America
Average Height: 14.3 to 16 h.h.
Aptitudes: Racing and riding

As Thoroughbred racing gradually became more popular than Quarter Horse racing, the Quarter Horse might have fallen by the wayside. It was soon discovered, however, what superb cattle horses they made, and over the years their cattle sense has been brought to an incredible level. They are quick and agile, and can turn on a dime and be up to full speed in no time flat. They are an excellent all-round horse, able to turn their hand or 'hoof' to anything. This breed is by far one of the most numerous in western Canada and the United States, and is thus very likely to be seen grazing in fields.

Quarter Horses are most easily recognized for their extremely well-developed hindquarters. Their heads are small and straight in profile, with small ears and wide-set eyes; neck muscular; withers prominent, with a short back; chest very broad and muscular; legs also very muscular; hooves quite small and hard; color solid, with white markings on face and legs common.

American Saddlebred

Originally known as the Kentucky Saddler, the American Saddlebred was founded during the 19th century as a easy-gaited, comfortable yet showy horse for plantation owners to ride. Overseeing their vast plantations meant that they had to spend long hours in the saddle, and horses that could carry them all day smoothly and easily were extremely sought after. Descended from the mixture of Morgan, Canadians, Narragansett Pacers, Spanish horses and Thoroughbreds, the Saddlebred took the best features of all these breeds. The American Saddlebred is a five-gaited horse. The two extra gaits are the 'slow gait' and the 'rack,' both of which are high-stepping prances with each foot stalling in mid-air before being placed on the ground.

Origin: United States of America
Average Height: 15 to 16 h.h.
Aptitudes: Five-gaited riding horse

Saddlebreds have a fine head straight in profile; ears small and pricked; eyes large and wide set; neck arched; shoulders sloped; chest wide; back short and body compact; legs straight; pasterns long; tail set unusually high; appearance smooth over all; color solid, with white markings on feet and head common.

Anglo-Arab

Just as its name infers, the Anglo-Arab is a horse bred from Arabians and Thoroughbreds. Usually it is exactly half and half, meaning that the sire was full Arab or Thoroughbred and the dam was full blood of the other. It is bred all over the world today but originated in France, England and Poland during the second half of the 19th century. In France they have been bred quite methodically, alternating between Thoroughbred and Arabian sires over subsequent generations to keep the breed from taking on characteristics that are too much of one or the other. The Anglo-Arab is, in fact, becoming an independent breed in its own right in France, where they are now breeding Anglo-Arabs to Anglo-Arabs.

This breed, stemming from two famous horse breeds, makes exceptional sport and event horses. They combine the best traits from both breeds, to bring together strength, stamina and athletic ability. Anglo-Arabs are usually quite tall, making them exceptional jumpers. The profile of the head is usually straight; neck long and arched, set on prominent withers; shoulders sloped and girth quite deep; back short and croup straight; legs fine but strong and hard; coat any color.

Origin: France, England and Poland
Average Height: 15 to 16.3 h.h.
Aptitudes: Sport and riding horse

Andalusian

This renowned horse has influenced many different breeds all over the world, including the Lipizzaner, Alter-Real and Paso Fino. The origin of the Andalusian is generally thought to date back to the Moorish occupation of Spain. It was during this time, in 711 AD, that the North African Barb was brought to the Iberian Peninsula by the invading Arabs. The crossing of the Barb with the indigenous Spanish horses was one of the main factors in the evolution of the Andalusian. Throughout history there have been many attempts to refine the Andalusian toward an Arab type, and were it not for the few breeders clinging to the old type, the purity of this breed might have been lost. The Carthusian monks of Jerez played an important and crucial role in the breeding of the Andalusian. During the 15th century they devoted their time and considerable wealth to the preservation of pure bloodlines.

Origin: Spain
Average Height: 15.1 to 15.3 h.h.
Aptitudes: Riding, bullfighting

Andalusians are the famous horses seen in the bullfighting ring dodging horns and fury to carry their riders out of harm's way, parading and high stepping past an awe-inspired audience to taunt the bull again. It is from the Andalusian that breeds like the Quarter Horse acquired their amazing 'cow sense,' an uncanny ability to anticipate the movements and actions of cattle. The Conquistadors were mounted on Andalusians when they came to the Americas, and most North and South American breeds owe at least some of their ancestry to this great horse.

Powerful and agile, the Andalusian is noted for its high action and proud carriage. It has a distinctive head with a slightly convex profile; ears small and eyes expressive; mane and tail long and very thick; neck thick and arched and attached to well-sloped, wide shoulders; body compact, with straight legs and strong joints; tail set low; color predominantly gray, but bay and chestnut are often seen.

Arabian

Perhaps no other breed of horse has had as much influence on horses the world over as the Arabian. It is believed by the Mohammedans that 'the Arabian horse was created by Allah with a handful of the south wind so that it could fly without leaving the ground.' Some believe that the Arab was a different subspecies of horse, but gene testing has proven otherwise. Yet, despite the controversy over its origins, people have believed in the greatness of this beautiful horse for centuries. Born of the desert, and bred for centuries out of harsh, dry conditions, the Arabian developed as an animal with exceptional endurance and stamina. As lighter armor was invented, it became apparent that the fleeter, Arab-type horses were superior to the larger, heavier European mounts, and the worldwide demand for Arabian horses began to grow.

Origin: Middle East
Average Height: 14 to 15 h.h.
Aptitudes: Riding

Today Arabian horses are bred all over the world. Although they are no longer used as cavalry mounts and war horses, the sport of endurance riding has seen the Arab in the top of its class. They are indeed a graceful and lovely riding horse. This popular breed is easily identified by its unique appearance, and is common in the United States and Canada.

Arabians have a very distinctive head and neck carriage. Interestingly, they have one fewer dorsal vertebrae than other breeds. Their dished profile, large expressive eyes, and slim, highly arched neck are quite unique among the horse breeds. The head is small with a wide forehead; ears small and turned in at tips; shoulders sloped and chest deep; back short and croup very straight, with little or no slope; tail set high; legs slim and strong; hooves small and hard; coat any solid color, with white markings on face and legs quite common.

Argentine Criollo

Three hundred years ago the Spanish explorers brought their horses to South America. Those horses were primarily Andalusian, Barb, Arab and Sorraia. Many of those horses escaped during conflict with the peoples of South America, or were intentionally turned loose. Nevertheless, over those 300 years of roaming wild in harsh conditions, the Argentine Criollo, descendant of those Spanish horses, developed into a hardy, enduring horse.

Origin: Argentina
Average Height: 14 h.h.
Aptitudes: Riding

Many amazing feats of stamina are a testament to this stocky horse's mettle. In 1925-28, a 10,000 mile (16,100 km) trek was undertaken by a man with two Criollo geldings. They traveled this phenomenal distance over every environment imaginable, from Buenos Aires to Washington, DC!

Argentine Criollos are smallish, stocky horses; head small, with a straight or slightly concave profile; neck very short and muscular; back short and croup sloped; legs short and muscular; mane and tail quite thick; color primarily dun, with zebra stripes on the legs, and many other colors are common.

Banker Horse

The feral horses of the North Carolina Outer Banks have roamed the windswept sand dunes since the first Spanish explorers traveled to that area. Protecting the coastline from the onslaught of the Atlantic Ocean, the Outer Banks form a barrier of sand dunes that run for about 175 miles (280 km). It is difficult to imagine such a place capable of supporting the lives of many horses! Until quite recently the Banker Horses have been very isolated, and as a result they have changed little from their early Spanish ancestors. Like most wild horses, when left to themselves to develop and survive, they tend to do very well, nature being the surest way of creating a creature most adapted to its specific environment.

As a result of their harsh surroundings, Banker Horses have maintained a rather small size, and the sparse diet of salt grasses keeps them trim. Angular of body with a bushy mane and tail, these hardy little horses bear a strong resemblance to

Origin: United States of America
Average Height: 13 to 14.3 h.h.
Aptitudes: Riding

the Mustang. They have a small head and short neck; back medium length; croup sloped; legs strong and hard; color predominantly dun, buckskin, bay and brown.

Barb

A horse of great antiquity, the Barb has had a profound influence on horse breeds throughout the world. It originated along the Barbary coast of North Africa where it has existed for thousands of years. It was first tamed and used by the Berbers for battle because of its speed and agility over short distances and endurance over long distances. When the Moors invaded Spain during the 7th and 8th centuries, they brought their Barb horses, which in turn gave rise to the famous Andalusian breed. Over the years the Barb became firmly established in Europe, and as a result many breeds owe their origins to it.

Origin: North Africa, Algeria, Morocco
Average Height: 14 to 15 h.h.
Aptitudes: Riding

Barbs are maybe not the most handsome of horses. They have rather long, narrow heads with wide muzzles; neck medium length set on upright shoulders; back short and strong, with very sloped croup; legs long and hard, with strong joints; hooves small and narrow, usually rock hard; mane and tail long and flowing; color usually solid.

Brumby

While there is some confusion over the term, and the use of it, a Brumby is any feral horse in Australia. Originally Brumbies and Walers came from the same stock, but the latter stayed domesticated and was influenced by humans, and the former roamed the arid climate of the Australian continent and became stout, hardy horses. Of course, horses of all different breeding often escaped to join the Brumby herds, but the general characteristics of the Brumbies stayed the same. Unfortunately, horses are not native to Australia, and they often out-compete native fauna, causing extinction and endangerment of other species. It is standard practice to cull the Brumbies' burgeoning populations so that they do not overrun the entire ecosystem.

Origin: Australia
Average Height: 14 to 15 h.h.
Aptitudes: Riding

Much like the Mustangs of North America, Brumbies are usually wiry and tough with medium-sized heads that are somewhat coarse; neck short and muscular, set into fairly upright shoulders and a deep chest; back short and straight, with sloped croup and a low tail set; legs strong and wiry, with broad joints; hooves hard; color varies, as with most feral horse populations.

Camargue

In the south of France near the Rhone River delta is a place of wild marshes and swamps. The famous and unique Camargue horse, named after the region it inhabits (it is also called 'the horse of the sea'), has roamed since prehistoric times. As a result, it breeds very close in body type, so much so that it is often difficult to tell one individual from another. Camargue horses are usually born dark in color, but as they mature they invariably turn gray. Many explorers have traveled through the Camargue area and taken these small, wild horses back home. Consequently it is thought that the Camargue horse might have influenced many horse breeds throughout the world. Today Camargue horses are semi-wild, with their breeding only slightly controlled. They are often used by the local people to herd cattle, but they are generally left to themselves.

Camargues have a large, square head with big, dark eyes and short, wide ears; neck short and shoulders upright; back short and croup sloped, with a low tail set; body thickset throughout; legs strong and solid; hooves hard; color always gray as adults.

Origin: France
Average Height: 13.1 to 14.1 h.h.
Aptitudes: Riding

Canadian

If one were to see a Canadian and a foundation Morgan standing side by side, there would be little doubt as to the relationship between them. So remarkable is the resemblance that except for a slight difference in height and some feathering on the legs, one would assume that they are the same breed! The Canadian is a horse that originated in New France from the early French stock brought over to populate the colony in the 17th century. The Breton and the Norman, which were influenced by the Andalusian and the Dutch Fresian, were the main horses brought to New France. Over the years the Canadian horses came about from the different French foundation horses. They were formed and shaped by the climate, hard work and industry of a new colony.

Origin: Canada

Average Height: 14.3 to 16.2 h.h.

Aptitudes: Light draft, riding and driving

Noted for their great trotting abilities, the French-Canadian horses, as they were known, became increasingly in demand as good roadsters. Their driving stamina on the roadways and their strength and pluck for farm labor made them a great source for cross-breeding with other types of horses. Unfortunately they were drawn upon so widely that the breed itself almost suffered extinction. The Canadian horse's popularity in the United States is testament to its character. Although it is not often given credit for much of its influence, many breeds in the United States and Canada owe at least some of their parentage to this rarely noticed horse, including, some would say, a little bay stallion named Justin Morgan.

Canadians are a striking horse with a short head and small, fine muzzle, very wide-set eyes and small pricked ears; neck arched and thickly crested; shoulders sloped; chest broad; back short, with a deep girth and gently sloped croup; legs very strong and well muscled; mane and tail very thick and wavy; legs feathered; color usually black or bay.

Cape Horse

When the Dutch first settled in South Africa during the 17th century, they imported horses from around the world for farming and transportation. The Cape Horse thus was developed from the many different breeds of horse brought to the Cape of South Africa. Early on, the Cape Horse formed a distinctive type that was much praised, and was traded with India for military uses. As more and varied kinds of horses were imported to South Africa over the subsequent centuries, the original Cape Horse lost much of its distinctiveness as it was outcrossed with many other breeds. By the time World War II was over, there were very few remaining old-type Cape Horses. Attempts have been made to revitalize this breed, but the Cape Horse of today is larger and more refined than its ancestors. Among the influences on the Cape Horse were Thoroughbred, Javanese ponies, Andalusian, Friesian, Hackney, Cleveland Bay and Norfolk Trotter.

Origin: South Africa
Average Height: 14.2 to 15 h.h.
Aptitudes: Riding and light draft

Cape Horses have fine heads, wide-set eyes and medium-length ears; neck long and arched, with a thin throat latch; shoulders sloped and muscular; back short; hindquarters round, with a slightly sloped croup and high tail set; legs strong and clean; hooves very hard; color variable and usually solid.

Carthusian

Carthusians represent the purest blood line of the famous Andalusian breed. They are considered to be a side branch of the Andalusian, which without the careful and strict breeding of the Carthusian Monks of Spain would most likely have been lost to outcrossing or reabsorbed into the Andalusian breed. All of the Carthusian horses alive today can trace their lines back to one stallion, a horse by the name of Esclavo, who was said to have been perfect in every way. Interestingly enough, Esclavo had warts under his tail, and often a descendant that did not also have these warts was considered to be illegitimate!

Carthusians are like Andalusians in every way except that they are almost exclusively gray. The have beautiful heads with broad foreheads, large, expressive eyes, small, pricked ears and wide, flexible nostrils; neck arched and carried high and proud, set into a deep, wide chest and very sloping shoulders; back short and straight, with a rounded croup and powerful hindquarters; legs clean and strong, with short cannons and long, flexible pasterns.

Origin: Spain
Average Height: 15.2 h.h.
Aptitudes: Riding

Chickasaw

This breed is named after the Chickasaw Indians who brought them from Florida to the rest of North America during the 1700s. They are descended from the Spanish colonial horses, namely Andalusian, Criollo, Barb and Sorraia, and were much sought after by the settlers of Virginia and South and North Carolina, who traded with the Chickasaw Indians for the horses. It is thought that Chickasaws played an important role in the development of the Quarter Horse, and certainly their conformation points to some connection.

Origin: United States of America
Average Height: 14 h.h.
Aptitudes: Riding

Chickasaw horses have a short head with very wide-set eyes and short ears; necks short and thick, set into sloped, muscular shoulders; chest broad and girth deep, with a short back and stocky, compact body; croup sloped and hindquarters strong and well muscled; legs clean and straight, with well-defined joints; hooves round and strong; color bay, brown, chestnut, sorrel, gray, black, roan and palomino.

Cleveland Bay

One of the oldest English horse breeds, the Cleveland Bay can trace its roots back to the 17th century. It was then known as the Chapman horse, named after the traveling merchants who used the horses to carry their wares. During the late 18th century the Cleveland Bay was crossed with the English Thoroughbred to produce the Yorkshire Coach Horse, which was much sought after until the advent of motorized vehicles.

The Cleveland Bay is popular the world over as an outstanding carriage and coach horse. As its name suggests, the Cleveland Bay is always bay in color with dark points and sometimes dapples. As a result, these horses make beautiful teams because they are invariably the same color, and when under harness they become one harmonious whole.

Origin: England
Average Height: 15.2 to 16.1 h.h.
Aptitudes: Riding, driving and light draft

A medium-size horse, the Cleveland Bay has a fairly large head with a slightly convex profile; neck long, set on sloped shoulders; back medium length and girth deep; hindquarters fairly level and tail set high; legs quite short, with broad joints and strong hooves; color always bay with a small star on the forehead permitted; mane and tail sometimes shot with gray.

Colorado Ranger

In 1878 the Sultan of Turkey presented U.S. General Ulysses S. Grant with two beautiful desert stallions. One was an Arab and the other a Barb, and from these two sprung the breed known today as the Colorado Ranger. Within a single season of breeding the two stallions left an unmistakable mark on the horses of the Nebraska ranch to which they were loaned. As time passed, word spread of the outstanding horses being bred in Nebraska, and a sizable herd was purchased and brought to the Colorado range. An amazing diversity in coloring sprung from the breeding of the Colorado Ranger. Leopard spots and rain-drop patterns had never been seen in Colorado before! The horses also commonly had more traditional Appaloosa markings, such as spotted blankets and snowflake patterns.

Origin: United States of America
Average Height: 14.2 to 16 h.h.
Aptitudes: Riding

Colorado Rangers are always spotted. They tend to look quite like other cow horses such as the Quarter Horse. They have small heads and strong necks with wide shoulders and compact bodies; back short and hindquarters well developed; legs strong and muscular; hooves hard; coat has all Appaloosa colors and patterns.

Don

This extremely hardy and tough horse was developed on the steppes that border the Don River, between Kazakhstan and Ukraine. It was the horse traditionally used by the Cossacks, and in fact it was these intrepid mounts that the Cossacks rode when they repelled the advance of Napoleon's army during 1812-14. After the retreat of the French, owing in large degree to the mass deaths of their horses from starvation and exhaustion, the Cossacks then rode their hardy Don horses all the way back to Moscow! Since then the Don breed has changed a bit: it is taller, owing to infusions of Turkoman, Karabakh and Karabair, and more refinement and quality were the result of Thoroughbred and Orlov Trotter. Today the Don makes an excellent all-round riding horse with great powers of endurance.

Dons have medium-sized heads, with straight profiles and wide-set eyes; neck fairly long and straight, with prominent withers and a straight back; shoulders fairly upright and chest deep; hip deep and croup gently sloped, with high tail set; legs long and clean, with hard, strong joints and tough feet; color solid, often a golden chestnut with a metallic sheen.

Origin: Ukraine and Kazakhstan
Average Height: 15.2 to 16 h.h.
Aptitudes: Riding and light draft

Florida Cracker Horse

Like so many other horses in North and South America, the Florida Cracker Horse is descended from stock brought by the first explorers and colonists from Spain. Named for their riders, known as 'crackers' for the cracking sound that their cow whips made, the Cracker Horses were indispensable for cattle work because of their tirelessness and stamina. Lake Kissimmee State Park in Florida is one of the few places to see these small, rare horses—there are only about 150 of them—and there are also a few ranches where Cracker Horses have been kept pure.

Origin: United States of America
Average Height: 14.2 h.h.
Aptitudes: Riding

Much like the American and Spanish Mustangs, the Chickasaw and other Spanish descendants, Florida Cracker Horses are hardy and tough. They tend to be smaller than other types of Spanish horses, but lack nothing in their mettle. Cracker Horses were described in 1838 by the Conte de Castelnau as 'small, long haired and bright eyed, lively, stubborn, and wild.' Rather angular, the Cracker Horse has a smallish head and medium-length neck; back straight and body wiry, with a sloping croup; legs slight but tough; hooves strong; color varies.

Frederiksborg

A famed horse of the 18th century, the Frederiksborg is the oldest breed of Denmark. It was a result of a German-bred mare's cross to Spanish stallions, and the Spanish influence can be seen in the Frederiksborg's often convex profile. The breed is little known today because it was greatly diminished in the demands for its export to other countries. After the Royal Stud closed, owing to shortages of breeding animals, a few breeders kept the Frederiksborg alive. Breeding of the Frederiksborg began again in earnest in Denmark after the 1930s. Friesian, Oldenburg, Thoroughbred and Arab were used to augment the low number of pure Frederiksborg horses. Although they are not exactly the same as their popular predecessor, they can be found in great numbers throughout Denmark today.

Frederiksborg horses have mid-sized heads with straight or convex profiles, pricked ears and large eyes; neck medium length, with sloped shoulders and pronounced withers; back short and straight, with a broad, rounded croup; legs muscular and strong, with broad joints; hooves small and hard; color always chestnut, often with a flaxen mane and tail; white markings on face and legs common.

Origin: Denmark
Average Height: 15.1 to 16.1 h.h.
Aptitudes: Riding and light draft

Friesian

The Friesian of today has not changed since it was ridden to war carrying the weight of armored knights during the Middle Ages. In fact, it is not difficult to imagine these regal black horses harnessed in battle gear and awaiting the command to charge into a melee, like a hurtling black phantom with the sunlight glinting off its armored rider. During World Wars I and II the Friesian breed was brought close to extinction because the demand for horses was so great. Horses of great parentage were as essential as the others, and unfortunately, many horses did not survive those wars.

Origin: Holland

Average Height: 15 to 16 h.h.

Aptitudes: Riding, light draft and carriage horse

An ancient breed, the Friesian is named for its native Friesland in the Netherlands. It has been bred there for centuries with great care. The Friesian has not been at all influenced by the English Thoroughbred, and for the last two centuries it has been bred completely pure, so it has retained a remarkably distinctive appearance. Friesians have amazing trotting abilities, which they most likely inherited from the Andalusian influence during Medieval times. Extremely high action, where the heels of the front feet sometimes brush the elbows, is quite characteristic of Friesians. They are very popular in carriage events and circuses because of their enormous charisma and majestic bearing. These beautiful black horses are making a name for themselves in North America, and are easily recognized.

The Friesian has influenced many breeds throughout the world and there is no doubt that its popularity is growing again outside of its native Friesland. Very sturdily built, Friesians have a regal head and bearing; head long with straight profile; eyes large; ears small and pointed inward; neck thick and carried high; body compact; legs and hooves strong; mane and tail thick and wavy, with feathering on the lower legs; color is always black, with a small white star on the forehead allowed only on geldings and mares.

Gelderland

lthough no longer officially bred, the beautiful Gelderland horse—named for the Gelderland Province in Holland—has made a marked contribution to the development of the Dutch Warmblood. Gelderlands can still be found today because some breeders would not let the purebred line disappear. Originally bred as a carriage horse, the Gelderland was developed with the help of many different breeds, including the Norfolk Roadster, Friesian, Thoroughbred, Arab, Hackney, Oldenburg, Andalusian and Holstein. A good jumper, the Gelderland can be seen in riding events, holding its own with the great event horses.

Origin: Holland
Average Height: 15.2 to 16 h.h.
Aptitudes: Driving and riding

The Gelderland is a fairly large horse that carries itself with grace and style, whether harnessed and pulling a carriage with a high-stepping trot or being ridden for show or pleasure. The head is longish with a straight profile; neck long and well muscled; back straight, with prominent withers and a short flat croup; tail set high; chest broad; legs muscular; hooves large; color usually chestnut, but sometimes bay, black and gray and very occasionally skewbald; white markings quite common on face and legs.

Guanzhong

The Guanzhong area in China has an interesting breed of horse whose roots are almost exclusively from outside of China. The people needed a horse strong enough to help in the agriculture of the region, and they imported stallions from different parts of eastern Europe, namely the Karabair, Budyonny, Ardennes and Soviet 'High Blood.' The result was a horse of endurance and strength. Guanzhong horses are used today for the improvement of other breeds and to fill their traditional role as light draft and riding horses.

The Guanzhong has a medium sized head with a straight profile and small muzzle; neck medium length, with slight cresting; back straight and rounded; hindquarters muscular; legs straight, with muscular forearms; hooves medium sized; color usually chestnut and bay.

Origin: China
Average Height: 14.3 to 15 h.h.
Aptitudes: Riding and light draft

Hanoverian

The Hanoverian is perhaps the most well-known horse breed in show jumping and dressage around the world: its achievements in equestrian events are legendary. Competition at the Olympic and professional level in show jumping and dressage is grueling for both horse and rider, and it takes exceptional individuals to compete. The Hanoverian horse was originally developed in Germany by the House of Hanover. Since then, the Hanoverian has been influenced by Holstein, Andalusian, Neopolitan, Thoroughbred and Trakehner. Nowadays breeding of Hanoverians is strictly controlled to ensure that only the highest standards are met. In Verden, Germany, each year, people come from all over the world to purchase top-class Hanoverians and other outstanding horses.

Origin: Germany
Average Height: 15.3 to 17 h.h.
Aptitudes: Riding and events

There a few types of Hanoverians of varying size and capabilities, but the commonly known show jumpers that thrill audiences worldwide are large elegant warmbloods of great athletic abilities whose leg action is ground covering and very elastic. Hanoverians are sometimes a little plain through the head; profile usually straight; neck long and muscular; shoulders powerful and sloped; girth deep; back medium length; hindquarters powerful; legs muscular, with large joints; hooves hard; color solid, with white markings common.

Hackney

A larger version of the little Hackney pony, the Hackney horse is well known for its spectacular action and beautiful carriage. Used today mainly as a show and exhibition horse, the Hackney was essential to England, where it originated. It was a roadster and coach or carriage horse until the advent of the railways. The Norfolk Trotter and Yorkshire Hackney were the early predecessors of the modern Hackney, and both of them were influenced by the Dutch Friesian. Thoroughbred and Arabian introduced to the early English trotters led to the development of the Hackney horse.

Origin: England
Average Height: 14 to 15.3 h.h.
Aptitudes: Harness and driving

The first Hackney to travel to the United States, during the early 1800s, was a stallion named Jary's Bellfounder, who by way of a mare that he sired had an important influence on the development of the Standardbred. By far one of the most popular attractions to show rings around the world, Hackneys are enjoyed by people everywhere.

Hackneys have a small head and muzzle with small, pricked ears; neck longish, arched and carried high on broad, sloped shoulders; body compact; back and croup straight; tail set high; hindquarters well muscled; legs medium length, with long pasterns; hooves hard; color predominantly bay, chestnut, sorrel, brown and black; white stockings and face markings common.

Holstein

The Holstein is a somewhat heavier riding horse than the Hanoverian, but has many of the same characteristics because the Holstein was one of the foundation sires for the Hanoverian breed. Following the Holstein's ancestry back through time, you would find the Great Horses of Medieval times, which can take credit for the existence of many modern horse breeds. Originating in Germany and developed from Andalusian and Oriental stallions bred to native mares, the Holstein gradually changed to a lighter coach horse as the need for chargers decreased and as the Cleveland Bay had a large influence. Thoroughbred blood was later introduced to bring the Holstein more toward a riding horse of great versatility.

Today Holsteins are world-class competitors in equestrian events, and there have been many famous Olympic and world-class champions of the Holstein breed. They can be seen in the show jumping ring, the eventing courses and the dressage ring. Holsteins have an expressive head, with a straight profile and large eyes; neck long, well muscled and arched; shoulders deep and sloped; back medium length and girth deep; croup fairly short and a bit rounded; legs medium length, muscular and dense; hooves hard and largish; color solid, bay is most often seen.

Origin: Germany
Average Height: 16 to 17 h.h.
Aptitudes: Riding and eventing

Kladruber

he Kladruber horse of the Czech Republic and Slovakia is akin to the Lipizzan in that its roots trace back to the old Spanish and Italian horses of centuries ago. There are two types of Kladruber found today: the White or Gray Kladruby, and the Black Kladruby. The Kladruby Grays are famous for pulling the state coach on ceremonial occasions, where the high, elegant action that they inherited from their Spanish ancestors is gloriously apparent.

Origin: Czech Republic and Slovakia
Average Height: 16.2 to 17 h.h.
Aptitudes: Driving and carriage horse

Kladrubers are a rare breed. They are late to mature and have a great endurance. Resembling the Andalusian, they have a regal head with a definite convex profile, large eyes and medium-sized ears; head carried high; neck arched and muscular, set into sloped shoulders and a longish back; croup round and tail set high; body compact and chest broad; legs strong and clean, with short cannons and large feet; color is always either white (gray) or black.

Knabstrup

Knabstrups are the national breed of Denmark, claiming direct ancestry to the horses of the Viking age. A church fresco in Denmark dating back to 1000 AD portrays a spotted horse. One of the main influences on this breed was a spotted mare left in Denmark by a Spanish officer. This mare left an indelible mark on the Knabstrup breed. It is likely that the Appaloosa and other spotted horses around the world are related in some way to the Knabstrup horses of Denmark. Today Knabstrup breeding is more popular, but modern breeders have aimed more toward color than for a type of conformation. The result is that the Knabstrup can be seen in a variety of shapes and sizes, including ponies!

Because of the lack of a common body type, the description of the Knabstrup is based mostly on their spots, which come in a variety of colors. They are usually solidly built and strong, with dense legs and hard hooves.

Origin: Denmark
Average Height: 15 to 16 h.h.
Aptitudes: Riding

Lipizzan

The famous Lipizzan horses of the Spanish Riding School in Vienna are beautiful white horses whose acrobatic feats and aerial leaps are reminiscent of the carousel horses that we all loved as children. Originally from Austria, the Lipizzaners are named after the village of Lipizza, which was part of Austrian territory during the development of the breed. The blood lines of the Lipizzan breed can be traced to the Spanish Andalusian and an Arabian stallion named Siglavy. Today Lipizzaners are bred in many countries, but Austria still claims the most notable stud. Only the Lipizzan stallions are trained for places like the Vienna Riding School. They tend to mature quite slowly; stallions in their 20s are often still performing. The training of Lipizzan stallions is a very long and careful task, undertaken with the utmost patience. It is the older experienced horses that train young riders and the older experienced riders that train the young horses. The combination of horse and rider is nothing short of an art form, and audiences around the world sit spellbound as these snowy white horses pass before them, performing their elegant movements.

Origin: Austria
Average Height: 15 to 16 h.h.
Aptitudes: Riding

Lipizzans are often born dark in color, changing to gray or white only later in their lives. They have fairly long heads with a straight or convex profile; eyes large; ears small; neck medium length, arched and muscular, set on sloped shoulders and low withers; chest wide and girth deep; back long and croup slightly sloped; tail set high; legs clean, with large joints; hooves strong.

Lusitano

The Lusitano is known to come from Andalusian stock, but beyond that there is uncertainty as to what other influences it might have had. The breed originated in Portugal, where it is well known as a mount for the Portuguese-style bullfighting done entirely from horseback. It is considered to be a terrible disgrace for the horse to ever be touched or injured by the bull. Lusitanos were also used as cavalry horses, and they can be seen today in dressage competition.

The Lusitano has a showy action that is much like its close cousin, the Andalusian, though not as high. Lusitanos have small heads with straight profiles, large, expressive eyes and small ears; neck rather short, thick and well crested; shoulders very sloped and withers low; back short and straight, with a rounded croup; chest broad and girth deep; legs medium length, clean and strong; color usually gray, but other solid colors seen as well.

Origin: Portugal
Average Height: 15 to 16 h.h.
Aptitudes: Riding

Mangalarga Marchador

The most popular horse in Brazil is the Mangalarga Marchador. It is the result of a mixture of Alter-Real, Andalusian, Jennet and Criollo, which makes it an excellent all-round horse. The Mangalarga is known for its fast, ambling gait, which is unique to the breed. The gait, called the 'marcha,' is thought to come from the famous Jennet horses of Spain, a now-extinct strain of Andalusian that was famous for its smooth, ambling gait. The 'marcha' is an exceptionally smooth and comfortable gait that covers a great amount of ground. Mangalarga Marchadors are also renowned for their cattle-working abilities.

This breed has a long head with a straight profile, wide forehead with large eyes and a small muzzle; neck arched and muscular, nicely set on strong, sloping shoulders and prominent withers; back short and croup long and slightly sloped; legs long, with plenty of bone; mane and tail fairly thin; color usually bay, gray, roan and chestnut.

Origin: Brazil
Average Height: 14.2 to 15 h.h.
Aptitudes: Riding

Missouri Fox Trotter

This breed was developed during the 1800s from a variety of American saddle horses, including Morgan, Arab and Thoroughbred, which were brought to Missouri with new settlers. The extremely comfortable gait for which the breed was named is said to be the easiest to ride over the rough, forested hills of the Missouri Ozarks. These horses are known for their surefootedness, and they make excellent trail and long-distance trekking horses because they are so comfortable to ride. The 'fox trot' is a very smooth sliding gait where the front feet walk quickly and the hind feet trot.

Origin: United States of America
Average Height: 14 to 16 h.h.
Aptitudes: Riding

Fox Trotters have a lovely head, set on a rather low-slung neck; shoulders sloping, with well-pronounced withers; back short and strong; croup round and muscular, with a high tail set; legs solid with well-defined joints and tendons; hooves round and of medium size; color includes black, bay, chestnut, gray, piebald and skewbald.

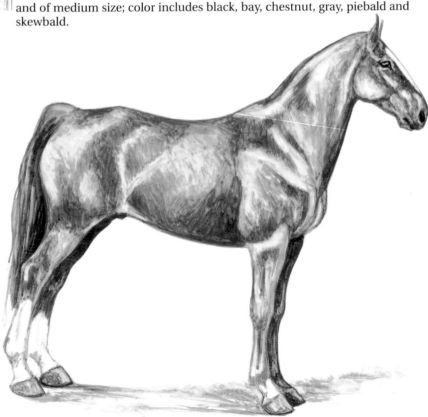

Morab

The Morgan and the Arabian are both popular horse breeds. They are both enduring and versatile, and so it stands to reason that a horse breed developed by crossing the two would be very successful. People began crossing Morgan, Arab and some Quarter Horses during the 1800s, and the resulting offspring combined all their best qualities. The famous Morab stallion Golddust is known to have had a very marked influence on this breed.

Morabs have beautiful heads, very reminiscent of Arabs, with large eyes and small ears; neck arched and muscular, set on sloping shoulders and a straight, short back; croup quite straight and tail set high; chest broad and girth deep; legs strong, with large joints and muscular forearms; hooves hard and round; color solid, and white markings on head and feet are not uncommon.

Origin: United Sates of America
Average Height: 14.1 to 15.2 h.h.
Aptitudes: Riding

Morgan

In 1789, a small bay stallion was foaled in Massachusetts. Named Figure, he became better known as Justin Morgan, after his second owner. Most people considered him too small to be of much use, until it was discovered how incredibly strong and durable he was. In an astonishing story of how he proved his great worth, there was a huge log that lay only a small distance to the mill, and which, despite many attempts by other teams of horses to move it, would not budge. The man who was in charge of Justin Morgan made a wager that his little horse could pull the log to the mill, and with three large men sitting on top of it, no less! The small bay stallion successfully moved the log in only two pulls, after having worked hard in the fields all day. Justin Morgan passed on his remarkable strength, endurance and mettle to all his offspring, and thus the Morgan horse breed was born. Quite common in North America, the Morgan is often seen in the country.

Origin: United States of America
Average Height: 14 to 15.2 h.h.
Aptitudes: Riding, driving and light draft

The origins of Justin Morgan are vague. He is generally thought to have been sired by a Thoroughbred out of an Arab mare, but he could also have had other influences in his blood lines. Canadians, Friesians, Norfolk Trotters, Norwegian Fjords and Welsh Cobs all have traits common to Morgans. Morgans today are a bit taller and more refined because they are used more for riding and driving than farm labor, but they are unmistakably cast in Justin Morgan's image. Morgans are admired and enjoyed widely for their great versatility, stamina and good-natured disposition. Morgans have beautiful heads, with small ears and large, wide-set eyes; head carriage high; neck thick and crested; body compact, with short back and powerful hindquarters; legs fairly short, but strong; mane and tail long and often wavy; tail set low, but usually carried higher; color solid, but never white.

Mustang

Mustangs figure prominently in American history, and stories—some famous, some untrue—tell great tales about these fleet and spirited wild horses that roamed the West. Descended from the Spanish colonial horses and then colored with all manner of horses that broke loose or were released to run wild, the Mustangs invariably bred naturally to a specific type. Today few Mustangs roam free; many were rounded up and broken for riding and many were slaughtered for meat. In 1971, a law was passed that protected the Mustang throughout the United States, and so the true spirit of the Mustang will always live on.

Origin: United States of America
Average Height: 14 to 15 h.h.
Aptitudes: Riding and light draft

Wiry and tough from their wild existence, the Mustang tends to be small and agile. The head is medium sized with small ears and wide-set eyes; neck medium length, well set into sloped shoulders and prominent withers; back short and croup sloped, with strong hindquarters and tough, hard legs and feet; color varies.

Namib Desert Horse

The Namib Desert of Namibia, Africa is an unrelenting, harsh landscape of rocky plains, mountains and rolling sand dunes. It is a wonder that this group of feral horses—which numbers only about 250 to 300 individuals—could survive in such an extreme climate and desert environment. Mystery surrounds the origins of these horses. One story attributes their existence to a shipwreck of Thoroughbreds that somehow survived and adapted to desert life. In another explanation, a German baron who built a castle in Namibia and who imported Trakehners from his native Germany had to abandon his estate, and the herd of horses left there survived to become the Namib horses. Whatever the ancestry of these unique horses, it is clear that they have become supremely adapted to their environment.

Namib Desert Horses are homogeneous in their appearance because they have been so isolated from other horses. They are very beautiful, with lovely heads, large, widely spaced eyes, dainty muzzles and small ears; neck long, with prominent withers and a short back; shoulders sloped and girth deep; croup gently sloped and tail set high; legs dense and very straight and clean, with remarkably hard hooves; color usually bay and sometimes brown and chestnut.

Origin: Namibia
Average Height: 14 to 14.3 h.h.
Aptitudes: Riding

National Show Horse

Developed from a combination of Arabian and Saddlebred, the National Show Horse is fairly recent breed that is becoming popular. It takes the beauty, stamina and refinement of the Arab and combines it with the high-stepping flare of the Saddlebred. The National Show Horse Registry opened in 1981 and includes horses that must be sired by either a pure Arab, Saddlebred or a National Show Horse. The dam must be also one of those three, bred to the opposite stallion if she is Arab or Saddlebred. This breed has two extra gaits, the 'slow gait' and the 'rack,' which are both animated four-beat gaits that are very comfortable to sit.

Origin: United States of America
Average Height: 15 to 16 h.h.
Aptitudes: Riding

The National Show Horse has a lovely head much like Arabs, and it combines the classic Arab conformation with the long, slender neck of the Saddlebred; head small, with large, wide-set eyes and medium-sized ears; neck very long and upright, with a slight arch; withers well set into a straight, short back, with a level croup and high tail set; hindquarters smooth and strong; girth deep and shoulders sloped; legs fine and straight; color varies, broken or solid.

National Spotted Saddle Horse

This breed originated in the latter half of the 20th century in Tennessee. Developed from Tennessee Walking Horses, American Saddlebreds and Standardbreds, the National Spotted Saddle Horse has spread out to much of the United States. The National Spotted Saddle Horse Association was formed in 1979. The breed is very popular with hunters and pleasure riders who admire its even temperament and surefooted, easy gaits. It is known for the 'rack' gait, at which it is most often seen.

The National Spotted Saddle Horse has a small head with intelligent eyes and small ears; neck short and thick, well set on sloped shoulders; body stocky, with powerful hindquarters; legs sturdy, with dense bone; color must be pinto to be registered.

Origin: United States of America
Average Height: 15 h.h., though many are smaller
Aptitudes: Riding

Nonius

In 1816, a stallion by the name of Nonius Senior was brought to Hungary to the Mezohegyes stud. He was of Anglo-Norman and Norfolk Roadster descent, and he lived in Hungary for a very long time, passing along his genes in his many offspring. The mares that he was bred to were mainly Spanish-Neapolitan, and they left an indelible mark on the Nonius breed. Thoroughbred was later introduced to add refinement. There are two types of Nonius: one is larger and goes by the name Hortobagyi Nonius. Used mainly in harness, the Nonius also makes an excellent sport horse when crossed with Thoroughbred.

Origin: Hungary
Average Height: 14.2 to 15.3 h.h. (small); 15.2 to 16.3 h.h. (large)
Aptitudes: Light draft and riding

The Nonius is a powerful, proud-looking animal with a large head, convex in profile, and large, expressive eyes; neck arched and of medium length, with a fairly upright shoulder and deep chest; back straight and wide; croup broad and sloped, with a low set tail; hip long and hindquarters powerful; legs long and clean, with broad joints and short cannons; hooves medium sized and strong; color principally black and bay.

Oldenburg

Considered to be the largest and perhaps the best known of the German warmbloods, the Oldenburg was founded about 300 years ago by Count Von Oldenburg. Originally used as a coach horse, the Oldenburg was based on the heavy Friesian with lighter blood from Spanish horses, Barb, Neapolitan and English Halfbred. It was later improved with Cleveland Bay, Thoroughbred and Norman blood. As the demand for coach horses decreased with the advent of motorized vehicles, the Oldenburg was yet again refined with infusions of Thoroughbred, Hanoverian and Trakehner. It is now an all-purpose riding horse that has begun to make a comeback in driving and harness events.

Oldenburgs have a rather large, plain head, sometimes with a Roman nose, and medium-sized ears; neck medium length and thick, set on well-muscled, sloped shoulders; back medium length and croup rounded with a high tail set; girth

Origin: Germany
Average Height: 16.1 to 17.2 h.h.
Aptitudes: Riding and driving

deep, though body tends to be flat-ribbed; legs short, with large joints and dense bone; hooves well shaped; color usually brown, black, bay and sometimes gray.

Orlov Trotter

The Orlov Trotter was the best trotter in the world before the development of the Standardbred. Count Alexius Girgorievich Orlov, who lived during the 1700s, was the founder of the Orlov Trotter. Count Orlov helped Catherine the Great take over the Russian throne from Peter III, and for his support he was promoted to commander of the Russian fleet. During the course of his career as commander, Count Orlov was presented with an Arab stallion named Smetanka by an admiral of the vanquished Turkish navy. When this stallion was bred to a Dutch Friesian, the resulting offspring became the foundation for the famous Orlov Trotter. As breeding began, the original stud had a mixture of different mares and all were used in the development of the great trotter.

Origin: Russia
Average Height: 15.1 to 17 h.h.
Aptitudes: Driving, draft and riding

Orlov Trotters have clean-looking heads with an Arab-like refinement, large eyes and small ears; neck long, fairly muscular and set high on rather straight shoulders; back long and straight, with a rounded croup; hindquarters powerful and girth deep, with well-sprung ribs; legs clean and dense, often with feathering on lower limbs; color usually a dappled gray, but black, bay and chestnut can also be seen.

Persian Arab

The Persian Arab is thought to be 1500 years older than the Arab of Arabia. A horse of unsurpassed stamina and endurance, its roots go back to the predecessor of the Arab itself. The Persian Arab is a beautiful horse, usually larger in stature than the Arab and often with a straight profile instead of a concave one. A small population of Persian Arabs called Asil Horses is considered to be of immensely pure blood lines. Asil mares almost always carry their foals to several days under the 11-month gestation period. Any foal not born in this time frame is considered to be less pure!

Very closely resembling the Arabian, the Persian Arab has a small head, with large, expressive eyes, small, pricked ears and a fine muzzle; profile either dished or straight; neck long and finely arched, with

Origin: Iran
Average Height: 14.1 to 15.1 h.h.
Aptitudes: Riding

sloped shoulders and a deep chest and girth; back short and croup straight, with a high tail set; legs long and fine, with hard bone and small, extraordinarily hard feet; color usually gray, bay and chestnut, and rarely black.

Paso Fino

'Paso fino' is the name of the slow, distinctive four-beat gait that all Paso Fino horses are born with. The beautiful, proud Paso Fino horse so well known in Central and South America is believed to be descended from the now-extinct strain of Andalusian, the Spanish Jennet, a horse breed that also exhibited a broken gait. Spanish Jennet mares were thought to have originally been bred to Andalusian stallions, and the resulting horse eventually became the Paso Fino. The fact that the four-beat gait of the Paso Fino is inherited and not learned is a testament to its individuality. The 'paso corto' and 'paso largo' are also four-beat gaits unique to this breed, and they are both faster than the 'paso fino'. These gaits are all extremely comfortable to sit. Throughout Central and South America the Paso Fino is known by many different names, such as Trochadores, Peruanos and American Paso Fino. Each of these names relates to a slight difference in conformation, so Paso Finos can take on a variation in size and shape, but all of them retain the unique gaits.

Origin: Puerto Rico
Average Height: 14 to 15 h.h.
Aptitudes: Riding

The Paso Fino is medium sized and lively. It has a small head with a convex profile and very large, wide-set eyes; neck medium length, arched and set upright on sloped shoulders; back medium in length, with well-developed hindquarters; legs fine and straight; hooves small; mane and tail very full and long; color solid.

Peruvian Paso

L ike so many of the horse breeds developed in South America, the
Peruvian Paso is descended from the different types of Spanish
horses brought to that continent during the 15th, 16th and 17th centuries. Subsequent introduction of several Old World breeds, such as the
Arab, Thoroughbred and Friesian, has added to the foundation for
today's Peruvian Paso. Much like the Paso Fino, the Peruvian Paso is born
with a four-beat, broken gait, which is very comfortable and can cover an
amazing amount of ground. A speed of 11 mph (18 km/h) can be steadily
maintained over uneven ground!

Origin: Peru
Average Height: 14 to 15.2 h.h.
Aptitudes: Riding

The Peruvian Paso is very animated with
its front feet, while its hind feet follow at a
lower step. It has a smallish head, with a
small muzzle and pronounced jaw; neck
thick, arched and short, with a thick
throat latch; shoulders fairly sloped and
back short; croup sloped and hindquarters muscular; legs straight and
well muscled; hooves hard; color solid, with chestnut and bay being the
most common.

Rocky Mountain Horse

The Rocky Mountain Horse is closely related to the Tennessee Walking Horse and the American Saddlebred. It is born with a very similar four-beat gait that makes for an incredibly comfortable ride. These horses have been used extensively in the Appalachian Mountains on farms, and they are well known for their extreme gentleness. The sire of this breed was a stallion named Old Tobe, who lived into his late 30s, carrying inexperienced riders through the mountains on trail rides. It is said that all of the Rocky Mountain Horses alive today carry some of Old Tobe's blood!

Origin: United States of America
Average Height: 14.2 to 16 h.h.
Aptitudes: Riding

Because of their easy, broken gait, Rocky Mountain Horses make excellent endurance riding horses. They are able to withstand harsh climates with little care and can travel at between 7 to 16 mph (11 to 26 km/h) without tiring. The breed has a medium-sized head, straight in profile, with large eyes and lively ears; neck well shaped and arched, set onto sloped shoulders and a wide, deep chest; back medium length and croup rounded, with tail carried fairly high; legs sturdy, with large joints and strong feet; color predominantly dark chestnut, with flaxen or blond mane and tail, but other solid coat colors are seen.

114

Shagya Arabian

Much like the desert-bred Arabian horses, the Shagya Arab, which is a more recent breed, is named for its foundation sire, Shagya. Shagya was a purebred Arab imported from Syria to Hungary in 1836. Although it is not of completely Arab origin, the Shagya is very close in appearance to pure Arabs. The main difference is that the Shagya is overall a much larger and more robust horse than its slighter, desert-born cousin. It is used primarily for riding and sometimes put in harness to pull light carriages.

The Shagya has a beautiful Arabian-shaped head, with large, expressive eyes, small ears and dished profile with a small, delicate muzzle; neck long and gracefully arched, set onto sloped shoulders; back medium length and croup level and slightly rounded, with a high tail set; barrel not as deep as some horses but ribs well sprung; legs strong and straight; hooves small and hard; mane and tail fine and silky; color usually gray, with the odd bay, chestnut or black.

Origin: Hungary
Average Height: 15 to 16 h.h.
Aptitudes: Riding and light harness

Sable Island Horse

About 100 miles (160 km) off the east coast of Nova Scotia lies an island that is about 20 miles (32 km) long and crescent in shape. It is a wind-swept sand dune that has been the bane of many ships and sailors who have lost their lives on the treacherous sandbars that sweep out from the island like great tentacles. The first record of a horse brought to the island is that of a Canadian stallion named Jolly. Many wild Sable Island horses resemble him. It is thought also that Spanish blood had an influence on these small, rugged horses, but just how all the horses prior to Jolly got there is open to debate. Most evidence suggests that they were brought there by a Boston merchant in the 18th century for the purpose of starting a farming settlement. Whether they were brought there by explorers or were shipwrecked and somehow managed to swim safely ashore, the horses of Sable Island have endured the hardships of life there for a long time.

Origin: Canada
Average Height: 13 to 14 h.h.
Aptitudes: Feral horse, ridden historically

Like all creatures left to themselves to survive in the wild, the Sable Island Horses have adapted to their environment: they have become small and sturdy, ideally adapted to the harsh, treeless landscape of Marram grass, blowing sands and frequent gale force winds. Their numbers are regulated by the food supply on the island and fluctuate year to year: anywhere from 200 to 360 individuals. They are one of three mammals that inhabit the island, including humans and seals. They have no natural predators and roam the island in small family bands of four to eight horses. A family group consists usually of a stallion, mares, their foals and some juvenile colts and fillies. Bachelor stallions form groups of their own, waiting for a chance to acquire their own herds by stealing another stallion's mares.

The Sable Island Horse is short and stocky, quick and agile, supremely adapted to racing around in the sand or up and down the hilly, grass-covered dunes. Its head is of medium size, with straight, convex and sometimes concave profiles; eyes large, often with distinctive mealy patches around muzzle; neck short and muscular; body compact; legs short and strong; feet unfailingly tough; color usually bay and many different shades of brown and chestnut; mane and tail usually long and full.

Standardbred

Harness racing is a sport popular all over the world. In fact, trotting races, where horses pull a cart instead of carry a rider, far precedes what we think of as horse racing, where the jockey clings to the back of a Thoroughbred as it thunders down the track. The name Standardbred comes from the standard time used to measure the time trials through which a horse had to go to enter a race. These speed trials over a distance of one mile (1.6 km) had to be completed in two minutes 30 seconds for a trotter, and two minutes 25 seconds for a pacer. Standardbreds are capable of trotting or pacing and, depending on the potential they exhibit as youngsters, they are trained in either gait. Pacing is often described as a rolling, piston-like stride with the legs on each side of the horse moving simultaneously together instead of in opposition.

Origin: United States of America

Average Height: 15 to 16.1 h.h.

Aptitudes: Harness racing and riding

The foundation sire for the Standardbred is a Thoroughbred named Messenger, imported to the United States in 1788. Messenger, through his descendant Hambletonian, had a profound influence on the Standardbred. Hambletonian was out of a Narragansett pacer mare, which would account for much of the Standardbred's trotting capabilities, as the Thoroughbred is primarily a galloper. Other infusions of Arab, Barb, Morgan, Canadian and Hackney also contributed to the Standardbred's stamina and style, but the main influence remains Thoroughbred.

Much like the Thoroughbred in appearance, the Standardbred differs in size and bulk. It is more heavily muscled than the Thoroughbred and is longer in the body. The head is less refined, with a straight or slightly convex profile, large flexible nostrils and somewhat long ears; neck straight and of medium length, set on sloped shoulders and a deep chest; back long and croup sloped, with very long, powerful, muscled hindquarters; legs fairly short, but immensely strong; hooves small and rock-hard; color usually bay, brown, black, chestnut and occasionally gray.

Tennessee Walking Horse

Claimed to be the most comfortable ride in the world, the Tennessee Walker is famous for its unique gait. It is like a running walk, where the front feet are raised straight and high and the hinds slide forward in an extremely long stride, overstepping the front tracks by up to 15 inches (38 cm)! The gait is basically a four-beat step, with the front feet running and the hind feet walking. The Tennessee Walker came about in Tennessee, where plantation owners needed a comfortable mount for long days in the saddle. Many consider the foundation sire of this breed to be a Standardbred by the name of Black Allan. He was born in 1886 and contained blood from the famous Hambletonian, as well as Morgan. Other influences, such as Thoroughbred, Narragansett Pacer, Saddlebred and Arab, also contributed to today's Tennessee Walker. Exhibiting great style and flare, this breed is both a wonderful sight to see and a charming ride.

Origin: United States of America
Average Height: 15 to 16 h.h.
Aptitudes: Riding

The Tennessee Walker has a medium-sized head, with a straight profile and longish ears. The head has a characteristic nodding when the horse is traveling at the running walk. The neck is strong, arched and carried upright; shoulders sloped and body compact; hindquarters rounded and powerful, with straight, clean legs and a very high tail set; mane and tail very long and full, usually worn loose; color solid.

Tersky

Tersky horses possess an amazing stamina and endurance. Looking very much like a large Arabian, the Tersky breed was started in the 1920s in an attempt to revitalize the Strelets Arab, which had almost died out after World War I. The Strelets Arab was not a purebred Arab—it carried the blood of the Don and Thoroughbred breeds, among others. The Tersky breed used the remaining Strelets as a foundation, with more Arab blood added. Thirty years or so later the Tersky was a fairly established breed that was bred often for steeple-chasing. Today, Tersky horses are still raced, but over flat distances against mostly Arabian horses.

With their large amount of Arab blood, the Tersky breed resembles purebred Arabians. Generally taller and more robust than Arabs, it has a fine head, with a straight or slightly dished profile, large, wide-set eyes and longish pricked ears;

Origin: Ukraine and Kazakhstan (Caucasus Mountains)
Average Height: 14.3 to 15.1 h.h.
Aptitudes: Riding

neck long and elegantly arched, with sloped shoulders and prominent withers; back short and broad; croup straight and fairly level, with a high tail set; girth deep; legs straight, clean and dense, with good feet; coat, mane and tail are thin; color usually a distinctive silvery gray, but chestnut and bay are also seen.

Thoroughbred

Perhaps the horse most known around the world is the Thoroughbred. Since its development, horse racing, which has existed for thousands of years, was brought to an entirely new level. The Thoroughbred is the fastest horse in the world over long distances. As the sport of Thoroughbred racing gained in popularity, Thoroughbreds were exported worldwide. The Thoroughbred can cover a mile (1.6 km) at nearly 40 mph (64 km/h)! They are supreme racing machines, and to stand on the edge of a track watching a group of racehorses thunder by is absolutely inspiring. The ground vibrates with the pounding of hooves, and the air is electric with the energy used to maintain the speed of the surging horses. Their jockeys cling to their backs like small, brightly colored beacons in a stormy sea of flying horse power.

Origin: England
Average Height: 15 to 17 h.h.
Aptitudes: Riding and racing

The lineage of modern Thoroughbreds can be traced back to all or one of the three great foundation sires of the breed. The Darley Arabian, the Byerley Turk and the Godolphin Barb (often referred to as an Arabian) were all imported to England during the late 17th and early 18th centuries and crossed with native mares. There are different types of Thoroughbreds according to the distances run. Sprinting races require a horse that is quick at the start, and so sprinters, needing to generate great speeds over short distances, are more compact and shorter than the longer distance runners. Long or middle distance race horses need stamina and endurance, and their tall, sleek physique and enormously long, ground-eating strides make it easier for them to cover more ground with less energy spent.

The modern Thoroughbred is a beautifully put-together horse. Its head is refined and expressive, with large eyes and medium-length ears; neck long and slightly arched, set into prominent withers and well-sloped shoulders; chest broad and girth deep to allow for greater heart and lung capacity; back short, with well-sprung ribs and muscular hindquarters; tail set high and croup gently sloped; legs strong, with length varying according to type; bone very dense and joints well developed, with flexible pasterns; hooves quite small and round, though tending to be brittle; skin very thin and fine; mane and tail fine and silky; color predominantly bay, brown and chestnut, but any solid color seen.

Trakehner

Originating in East Prussia and transferred to West Germany after World War II, the Trakehner breed has a colorful past. The foundation stock for the Trakehner is thought to be the native Lithuanian horses, descended from the horses of the ancient Sythians. The now-extinct Turkmenian and the Akhal-Teke blood would have figured prominently in the native Lithuanian horses. Infusions of Arab and Thoroughbred were later added to the horses bred at the stud in Trakehnen. World War II was disastrous for this fine breed, as it was for so many other breeds. The Trakehner is now bred all over Germany and is considered to be one of the best sport and competition horse breeds around.

Origin: West Germany and East Prussia
Average Height: 16 to 16.2 h.h.
Aptitudes: Riding and eventing

The Trakehner is a large horse with great athletic abilities. It has an elegant head, with a wide forehead and a graceful, muscular neck; shoulders well sloped and withers prominent; back short; hindquarters well rounded and strong; legs straight and hard, with short cannon bones and good feet; color usually solid, but occasionally piebald.

Waler

Walers were named for the place of their origin, New South Wales, Australia. The first settlers brought their livestock, including horses, primarily from Europe and South Africa. The horse breeds included, most commonly, Thoroughbred and Arab. As a result, the early Waler horses greatly resembled Anglo-Arabs, and they made saddle horses of great quality. During the 1850s and 60s, the gold rushes brought about the need for pack and draft horses instead of saddle horses, and so the Waler breed was somewhat neglected. In the 1880s attention once again turned to the Waler, and it was subsequently improved. No longer the same horse that it once was, Walers have good powers of endurance and make great all-purpose riding horses.

Owing to the variation in the appearance of the Waler, it can best be described as having a medium-sized head, longish ears and straight profile; neck well set on strong, sloped shoulders; back and hindquarters strong; girth deep; legs with plenty of bone; hooves strong; color solid.

Origin: Australia
Average Height: 15 to 16 h.h.
Aptitudes: Riding

Welsh Cob

Welsh Cobs are famed for their impressive trotting abilities. They are considered to have been the backbone of Wales before the first heavy horses were brought to the British Isles. Welsh Cobs were indispensable on the farms and in the forests; they were relied upon for a quick, strong mode of travel. Even during wars they were a substantial asset. The ancestry of the Welsh Cob is hazy, but they may have come from ancient Spanish stock, the ancestor to the Andalusian, which subsequently interbred with the native Welsh Mountain Ponies. Indeed, Welsh Cobs have a rather regal bearing and style.

Origin: Wales
Average Height: 14 to 15.1 h.h.
Aptitudes: Riding and light draft

The Welsh Cob has a small head, with bold, wide-set eyes and small, pricked ears, set onto an arched and muscular neck; withers pronounced and shoulder sloped; chest broad and deep; back short, broad and very strong; croup sloped and hip long, with round, muscular hindquarters; tail set high; legs fairly short, with strong, dense bone and well-defined joints; hooves very hard and of medium size; fetlocks feathered; mane and tail quite thick and often wavy; color solid.

Draft Horses

Ardennais

The Ardennais horse has had a long and convoluted history. This breed stems from the original war horses of the Middle Ages, often referred to as Great Horses, and was instrumental in the development of the Swedish and Belgian Ardennais breeds, to name only the obvious. It is thought that Napoleon used Ardennais horses to pull his artillery wagons during his military campaigns, and it was also used as a coach horse before it became so heavy. Today there are two types of Ardennais: a smaller, lighter version, probably more like the first Ardennais horses, and a heavy type. Both are exceptionally hardy and vigorous.

Origin: France
Average Height: 15 to 16 h.h.
Aptitudes: Heavy draft

The Ardennais heavy horse is massive on every level. It is compact and amazingly strong. The head is medium sized, with a broad forehead and large, kind eyes; neck immense and crested, set into a broad chest and sloped muscular shoulders; girth very deep and barrel round, with well-sprung ribs; back short and hindquarters sloped and enormous; legs very heavy and strong, with a large amount of feathering; hooves large and round; color usually roan, bay and chestnut.

Belgian Ardennais

Originating in the Ardennes region in Belgium and France, the Belgium Ardennais is thought to stem from horses that were prized by Julius Caesar. The Belgium Ardennais is very closely related to the original Ardennais, which is thought to have played a significant role in the creation of the Great Horses of the Middle Ages. The Belgium Ardennais is a larger version than the original because of some infusions of Belgian Heavy Draft blood. It is an extremely hardy horse with great endurance and is well known for its easy nature.

This horse is massive and compact, with a well-shaped head and small ears; neck thick and crested and relatively short; withers low and well defined, set into a short, wide back; shoulders well sloped and powerful, with a deep girth and very round barrel; hindquarters vast, with a sloped croup; legs short and very thick, especially through the hocks, with a good deal of feathering on the lower legs; hooves large, wide and very strong; color usually bay, roan, chestnut, gray and palomino.

Origin: Belgium
Average Height: 15.1 to 16.1 h.h.
Aptitudes: Heavy draft

Belgian Heavy Draft

The Belgian Heavy Draft is a lively and agile horse despite its great size and power. Also known as the Brabant, the Belgian most likely originated from the prehistoric heavy horses of the alluvial period (when the glaciers were melting from the Ice Age). This breed was well known during the Middle Ages, as were all of Belgium's heavy horses. The Belgian horses began to be bred in earnest during the late 1800s, when a uniform type was established. As a result these horses usually breed very true to type. The American Belgian is the North American version of this breed, and is most often seen in the United States and Canada.

Origin: Belgium
Average Height: 16 to 17 h.h.
Aptitudes: Heavy draft

A very large horse, the Belgian Heavy Draft can weigh over a ton (900 kg)! It has a rather small, well-shaped head and a short, thick neck that is heavily crested; body compact and robust, with massive hindquarters; back short and girth deep; legs short and muscular, with some feathering on the lower legs; color quite often a red roan with dark points, but chestnut, bay, brown, dun and gray also seen.

Boulonnais

The Boulonnais horses of northern France have existed there since the 1600s. Oriental blood was introduced to this breed during the Roman invasion of Britain, when Julius Caesar's cavalry was brought to the coast of Boulogne to await orders. During the Crusades, the Spanish brought their well-known Andalusian horses, the effect of which on the Boulonnais horse can still be seen today. There are two different types of Boulonnais: a small version, often referred to as the Petite Boulonnais, and the larger Boulonnais. Both types are gentle and active, although the former is now very rare.

The Boulonnais has a small head with a very broad forehead and small ears; neck thick and arched, with a very thick mane; chest wide and barrel round, with well-defined withers and a straight back; hindquarters round and well muscled, with strong legs and well-defined joints; lower legs sparsely feathered; color usually gray.

Origin: France
Average Height: 15.1 to 16.3 h.h.
Aptitudes: Heavy draft

131

Breton

The most popular of the draft horses in France, the Breton comes from the Breton Mountains, where it is thought to descend from the horses used by the Celts. These horses were later bred to Oriental stock brought to France during the Crusades, which lead to the Bidit Breton, a horse much sought after for its comfortable ambling gait. Subsequently, the Breton was influenced by Percheron, Boulonnais, Ardennais and Norfolk. Today the Breton has three types: the small Breton Draft, the Breton Draft and the Postier Breton. All three are very close in conformation, except for the size difference between the first two, and the Postier type having high, easy gaits and more style than the others.

Origin: France

Average Height: 15 to 16 h.h., depending on type

Aptitudes: Heavy and light draft

The Breton has a medium-sized head with a straight profile and wide forehead; eyes expressive and ears small; neck short and strong, well set into sloped shoulders and a deep chest; back short and wide, with round, powerful hindquarters; legs short and strong, with little or no feathering; color usually chestnut or chestnut roan, often with blond mane and tail.

Dutch Draft

The Dutch Draft horse closely resembles the Belgian Heavy Draft and the Belgian Ardennais because the blood from both of those heavy horses was used in the development of the Dutch Draft. It originated in Holland, where the local Zeeland horse was crossed with the two Belgian breeds. The result was a horse of great quality endowed with an amazingly calm and quiet disposition, as well as a characteristic slowness of movement. It is, however, quite capable of strong and lively movement when needed.

This breed is exceptionally massive in bulk, larger than any of the Dutch breeds. It has a small head, with a straight profile and small ears; neck short and heavily crested, set into very muscular shoulders and back; barrel round and very thick, with strong, sloped hindquarters; legs also heavily muscled and strong; hooves hard; lower legs feathered; color usually chestnut, bay or gray.

Origin: Holland
Average Height: up to 16.3 h.h.
Aptitudes: Heavy draft

Clydesdale

The Clydesdale originated in an area of Scotland near the Clyde River once called Clydesdale but now known as Lanarkshire. The need for a heavier horse to increase hauling power over the newly developed roads during the mid-18th century caused the local people to import larger horses to Scotland, such as the Belgian Draft and the Dutch Friesian. These large horses were bred to the native Scottish horses around the Clyde River area, and the resulting offspring became known as the Clydesdale. As word of the big and powerful horses in the Lanarkshire area spread to the rest of Scotland and then to Europe, the demand for the Clydesdale began to increase. They are now found throughout the world, and in the United States and Canada they enjoy great popularity. With their unique markings and large size, Clydes are easy to spot.

Origin: Scotland
Average Height: 16.1 to 18 h.h.
Aptitudes: Heavy draft

Perhaps the best known Clydesdales in the world are the Budweiser Clydes. They travel the world pulling the big Budweiser wagon, meeting millions of people each year. Budweiser Clydesdales are larger than the early Clydes of Scotland, standing 18 hands high and weighing about 2000 pounds (900 kg). They are all bay with four white stockings and a blaze. It is nothing less than spectacular to see the eight-horse hitch of these 'gentle giants' go cruising past, decked out in their beautiful harness and pulling the famous red Budweiser Beer wagon.

The Clydesdale has a large head with a convex profile and kind eyes; muzzle wide and ears long; neck massive and arched, set into slightly sloped shoulders and a broad chest; withers high; back short and wide, with sloped croup; hindquarters immensely strong; girth deep and barrel round, with well-sprung ribs; legs straight and strong, with large joints; lower legs profusely feathered; hooves broad and very tough; color usually bay with white stockings, but brown, black and roan also seen, and white markings on the face are very common.

Irish Draft

The Irish Draft is not a true heavy horse of the gigantic proportions that typically come to mind when we think of draft horses. It is tall and fairly large boned, but it is also known for its fluid movement and inherent jumping ability. It was developed by Irish farmers during the 18th century largely from the native ponies and horses of Ireland. They needed a horse that would be big enough to do farm work, but was also capable of being a reliable and agile mount or roadster. When this breed is crossed with Thoroughbred, the resulting offspring is invariably an exceptional jumper and eventing horse, which has come to be known as the Irish Hunter.

Origin: Ireland
Average Height: 15 to 17 h.h.
Aptitudes: Riding and draft

The Irish Draft has a proud head with a broad forehead, straight profile and long ears; neck medium length, arched and set into well-sloped shoulders and prominent withers; girth deep and back short, with a gently sloped croup; hindquarters powerful; legs clean and very hard, with short cannons; feet round and large; fetlocks slightly feathered; color usually gray, brown, chestnut and bay.

Italian Heavy Draft

The only draft breed from Italy, the Italian Heavy Draft was developed by crossing Breton stallions with local mares. The mares were of mixed breeding, including Hackney, Belgian Draft and Breton. The Italian Heavy Draft was used extensively by the Italian army to haul supplies and to produce stout mules needed for work. Mechanization and the rise of the automobile reduced the need for draft horses in Italy, as it did all over Europe, and the need for the Italian Heavy Draft declined. It is used primarily for meat production today.

Closely resembling the Breton, the Italian Heavy Draft is noted for its distinctive coloring, usually a liver-chestnut with flaxen mane and tail. It has a medium-sized head with a straight or convex profile, large eyes and small ears; neck short and thick, set into powerful

Origin: Italy
Average Height: 15 to 16 h.h.
Aptitudes: Heavy draft

shoulders and a short broad back; hindquarters rounded and sloped; girth deep and ribs well sprung; legs straight and clean, with feathers on lower legs; hooves strong and boxy; color may sometimes be roan and bay, with white markings on the face and legs common.

137

Jutland

The national draft horse of Denmark, the Jutland traces its roots to the Island of Jutland, where a horse of its type has existed for about 1000 years. The ancient Jutland horses were used by Danish knights as battle mounts during the Middle Ages, and quite possibly by the Vikings before that. Oppenheim LXII, a Suffolk-Shire stallion brought to Denmark in the late 1800s from Great Britain, left an indelible mark on the modern Jutland. Today it is possible to see Jutland horses in Copenhagen, where they have pulled the Carlsberg brewery wagons since the 1920s. They travel to many places, participating in shows and festivals and pleasing onlookers.

Origin: Denmark
Average Height: 15.2 to 16.1 h.h.
Aptitudes: Heavy draft

The Jutland has a medium-sized head, with kind eyes and long ears; neck short and crested, set into massive shoulders and chest; back long and broad, with a very deep girth, deeper in fact than the legs are long; hindquarters sloped and powerful; legs short and dense, with long feathers on lower legs; color most commonly chestnut, with light mane, tail and feathering, occasionally bay, black and roan are seen.

Lithuanian Heavy Draft

This widespread breed of Lithuania was developed from crossing the local Zhmud horses with Swedish Ardennais. This horse is large and coarse and well adapted to the extreme temperatures of its native Lithuania. It was used for farm labor and city transportation until mechanization reduced the need for it, but it is still found in large numbers throughout Lithuania.

This breed tends to be a bit coarse through the head, and the back is often dipped, but aside from that it is hardy and long-lived. The head is large and expressive, set on a very short thick neck;

Origin: Lithuania
Average Height: 15 to 16 h.h.
Aptitudes: Heavy draft

back long and broad, with a wide, sloped croup; legs well muscled, though hind legs are often sickle-hocked; feet strong and lightly feathered; color commonly chestnut, with blond mane and tail, but black, bay, roan and gray are also seen.

Noriker

The Noriker of Austria was named for the Roman kingdom of Noricum, today Austria, where it was thought to have originated. Andalusian and Neopolitan blood was introduced when the Church took an interest in the breeding of Norikers during the Renaissance. This breed is often strikingly spotted, especially among the Pinzgauer type.

Origin: Austria
Average Height: 16 to 16.2 h.h.
Aptitudes: Heavy draft

For roughly 2000 years, this horse breed has lived in the mountains of Austria, and it is supremely adapted to the rigors of alpine life. Because of the difficulty of maneuvering heavy machinery in the high, steep slopes, the Noriker is still used for draft work related to logging. With their small feet, Norikers are amazingly surefooted in a way that no other heavy breed can match.

The Noriker is stout and compact, with a large, plain head set on a short, thick neck; shoulders upright and chest broad; back long and broad, with strong hindquarters and sloped croup; legs fairly short, with large joints and little or no feathering in the lower leg; feet small and very sound; color often chestnut or bay, with flaxen mane and tail, but skewbald, spotted and dun are also seen.

Percheron

Based on the fossil record of the Le Perch area of France, a horse of Percheron type roamed there during the Ice Age. It is unclear what the exact origins of the Percheron are, but during the 8th century Arabian blood was introduced to the native horses of Le Perch. Often described as an overdeveloped Arab, the Percheron has a grace and elegance that is unmatched by the rest of the world's heavy draft breeds. It is perhaps the most widely distributed heavy breed in the world, finding favor for its great ability as a draft horse as well as for its style. If you see a huge black or gray draft horse in a field, chances are it's a Percheron.

The Percheron has a lovely head with a straight profile, wide forehead and slender ears; eyes large and expressive; nostrils wide and flexible; neck long and arched, with a slim throat latch; shoulders well sloped and chest broad and deep; back short and straight, with well-sprung ribs; croup rounded and sloped; hip deep and tail set high; legs clean and strong, with almost no feathering; color usually black or gray.

Origin: France
Average Height: 15.2 to 17 h.h.
Aptitudes: Heavy draft

141

Shire

Thought to be one of the purest descendants of the Medieval Great Horses, the Shire horse is well loved by its native England. It was a war horse, carrying armored soldiers over great distances and protecting them in pitched battle; a work horse for the docks of England, hauling the goods to and from the great ships that plied their trades all over the world; and a faithful farm horse that tilled the earth and transported agricultural products to the cities. The Shire was influenced by the Dutch Friesian when Dutch engineers came to England to drain the fens. The subsequent names of Lincolnshire Black and Old English Black, attributed to the Shire horses, account for the Friesian blood.

Origin: England

Average Height: can exceed 18 h.h.

Aptitudes: Heavy draft

Shires are the largest horses in the world, standing up to a height of 19 hands and weighing 2,600 pounds (1.2 t)! These immense horses epitomize the term 'gentle giants,' with their truly sweet personalities and their ability to pull a huge tonnage! Today Shires are no longer needed for their great hauling power to pull the commerce of England to and fro, but they are no less popular. Audiences at pulling contests and exhibitions the world over are sure to see the mighty Shire horses perform their colossal feats.

The Shire has a medium-sized head that is refined and aristocratic; profile slightly convex, with kind, wide-set eyes and slender ears; neck long, arched, with a strong crest, set into powerful, sloping shoulders; back broad and barrel round and deep; hindquarters rounded and strong, with a sloped croup and low tail set; legs quite long for a draft breed and well muscled, with large amounts of feathering on the lower legs; hooves large and round; color black, bay, brown and gray, with white markings on face and legs common.

Suffolk

Considered to be the oldest heavy breed in Great Britain, the Suffolk horse was used by the farmers of Suffolk who independently bred these stout horses. They have been nicknamed 'Suffolk Punch' because their fairly short legs appear to be too small for the great bulk of the body, and for their immense pulling capabilities. As a result of the isolation of the Suffolk area, they are very pure and breed true to type: Suffolks are always chestnut in color. All Suffolk horses can trace their ancestry back to one foundation sire, a horse foaled in the 1760s named Crisp's Horse of Ufford.

Origin: England
Average Height: 16 to 17.1 h.h.
Aptitudes: Heavy draft

The Suffolk is a medium-sized draft horse with a medium-sized head and large eyes and ears; neck muscular and crested, set into massive shoulders and chest; withers flat, with a deep girth and very round, dense barrel; hindquarters round and powerful, with a fairly high tail set; legs short, dense and clean, with short cannons and pasterns and no feathering; color is without exception one of seven different shades of chestnut.

Horse Types

American Paint

Looking as though a bucket of paint has been thrown at it, the American Paint horse is aptly named. The two basic patterns of the Paint horse are the 'overo' and the 'tobiano.' The tobiano horse has mainly a white coat with large, dark irregular patches usually on the head, neck, chest and flank. The overo horse has a dark coat with splashes of white covering the sides, neck and often the head. The American Paint Horse Association registers Paint horses primarily of Quarter Horse or Thoroughbred breeding. The horses must have broken patterns to qualify. Paint Horses make excellent stock horses owing to their Quarter Horse blood, and the Thoroughbred makes them an all-round great riding horse.

Origin: United States of America
Average Height: 15 to 16 h.h.
Aptitudes: Riding

The early Paints and Pintos, in North America at least, were descended from the first horses brought by Spanish explorers to South America, but horses with broken patterning have been around since before the first humans were making rock paintings. Indeed, in China and Egypt are ancient murals depicting spotted and patterned horses. The Natives of North America prized their Paint horses because they afforded better camouflage.

Because of the mainly Quarter Horse and Thoroughbred blood of the American Paint horses, they are usually a compact, stock-type horse with a straight profile and small ears; neck muscular set into sloped shoulders and a short, strong back; hindquarters very strong and well muscled; legs dense and muscular; feet small.

Albino

Wrapped in mythology, the white horse has often represented virtue and endurance. Knights and kings of old were always mounted on white horses, and the pure white horse often portrayed the prowess and greatness of military leaders. Napoleon always rode a white horse.

Origin: United States of America
Average Height: about 15 h.h.
Aptitudes: Riding

Although true albinism does not exist in horses, albino-like horses are called Albinos. Albino horses are marked by their absence of color, characterized by their pink skin and blue eyes. Albino horses originated in the United States, where a stallion of Morgan-Arab descent by the name of Old King is responsible for what is considered in that country an all-white breed. Albino horses do not conform to a specific body type, but are characterized by their coloring. White horses tend to be more susceptible to sunburn than dark horses, but it is not necessarily true that blue-eyed horses cannot see well.

Appaloosa

J ust like the Paint and Pinto horses that descended from the early
Spanish horses, so too were Appaloosas among the first horses to
repopulate the North American continent after the extinction of the
horse in North and South America during the last Ice Age. Spotted horses
are ancient. Evidence of their existence since the Ice Age can be seen in
cave paintings throughout the world. The development of the Appaloosa
horse in North America is attributed to the Nez Perce Indians, who lived in
what is now Washington, Oregon and Idaho. In fact, the name Appaloosa is
a derivation of the Palouse River in the State of Washington.

There are six different Appaloosa patterns: leopard, frost, spotted blanket,
white blanket, marble and snow flake.
Variations can be seen of all or one of
these patterns. The basic coat color is
most often roan but other colors are

Origin: United States of America
Average Height: 14.2 to 16 h.h.
Aptitudes: Riding

also seen, and the muzzle and around the eyes are usually mottled.
Appaloosas also display the characteristic white sclera around the eyes,
and usually have vertically striped hooves. Because Appaloosa horses are
a color breed, there is little conformity to a specific body type. Most
often, however, they have a Quarter Horse-like physique with a very thin,
wispy mane and tail sometimes referred to as a 'rat-tail' or 'finger-tail.'

Canadian Cutting Horse

The sport of cattle cutting is popular in western Canada and all over the United States. A horse and rider must separate a cow from a herd and work it for two and a half minutes without letting it run back to the rest of its fellows. A good cutting horse is not directed by the rider and displays remarkable cow-sense and a lightning agility. It must be able to out-think the cow and anticipate its movements. The Canadian Cutting Horse is not a breed, but a registry for cutting horses of a specific standard which establishes common rules for cutting competition. As a result, Canadian Cutting Horses can be any breed, but are most usually Quarter Horse because that breed out-performs most others in this event.

Origin: Canada
Average Height: 15 to 16 h.h.
Aptitudes: Riding

The ideal cutting horse should be absolutely calm and cool while working a cow and very economical in its movements, with quick bursts of speed to keep control of its chosen quarry.

Canadian Sport Horse

Much like the Canadian Cutting Horse Association, the Canadian Sport Horse Association was set up to promote excellence in the Sport Horses bred in Canada. Horses to be registered with the Canadian Sport Horse Association must pass stringent standards of endurance, athletic ability and jumping capabilities, and meet with correct conformation requirements. The registry is open to horses of any breed as long as they meet the standards, but it is conceivable that the Canadian Sport Horse could one day evolve into a breed in its own right.

This type of horse does not have a specific appearance, as it is a registry made up of many different breeds. Sport Horses in general are usually tall and athletic. They are built for endurance and jumping as well as dressage, so they must be very versatile. Conformation should be good and they should be very sound of hoof and leg.

Origin: Canada
Average Height: 16 h.h.
Aptitudes: Riding and eventing

Buckskin

The Buckskin, or Dun, can be of any breed. The prominent gene factor that produces dun-colored horses is thought to have been the most prevalent factor for color seen on prehistoric horses. Indeed, most of the ancient breeds that can trace their ancestry back purely to prehistoric horses, such as the Norwegian Fjord or the Sorraia of Spain, are predominantly dun. Dun coloring is characterized by a tan or sandy coat with black ears, legs, mane and tail, a black dorsal stripe and zebra striping on the legs and often the shoulder. The buckskin color is much the same, but without the dorsal and zebra stripes.

Origin: United Sates of America
Average Height: 15 h.h.
Aptitudes: Riding

The Buckskin and Dun horses in North America today descended from Spanish colonial horses, and because the gene that produces dun or buckskin coloring is dominant, there are many of these horses throughout Canada and the United States. Many people believe that Dun horses are sounder of hoof and have greater stamina and endurance than horses of other colors. If the dun gene harkens back to the prehistoric ancestors of the modern horse, then the hardiness of the ancient wild horses of the Ice Age could very well have passed on to the Dun horses of today. The American Buckskin Horse Registry is open to horses of any breeding as long as they are buckskin or dun.

English Hack

The term 'Hack' has been used to describe horses for hire, horses ridden purely for transportation and horses of refinement and elegance ridden by the upper crust of society. Nowadays, the English Hack is described as any horse used for leisure and pleasure riding, but there are stricter guidelines for the ideal 'show Hack.'

The English Hack of today is usually of Thoroughbred and Arab blood or Thoroughbred and pony mix. It should not be too tall and it should have extremely good manners as well as smooth and flowing gaits. It must be easy to handle and very well put together, showing refinement through the head and neck, with a well-sloped shoulder and good overall conformation. Judging of the show Hack is based heavily on how well trained a horse is.

Origin: England
Average Height: Must not exceed 15.3 h.h.
Aptitudes: Riding

English Hunter

Just as 'Hack' is a term used for any pleasure horse, 'English Hunter' describes any mount used for hunting. The traditional fox hunting of Europe saw the need for a large horse, capable of carrying a fair amount of weight over long, cross-country distances and many types of terrain, and able to jump over any obstacles. In competitions, modern Hunters are judged for their ability to carry the appropriate weight for their size and their degree of willingness to complete a course. Conformation is also a large factor, as it testifies to a horse's soundness for a season of hunting or competing. Most Hunters have Thoroughbred blood and many believe that a Thoroughbred and Irish Draft mix makes the best Hunter.

Origin: England
Average Height: 14.2 to 17 h.h.
Aptitudes: Riding and eventing

It is indeed an exciting sight to see a hunt set out for a day in the countryside, with the hounds running before the horses and the riders mounted in anticipation of the chase. All wait for the bray of the horn to announce the beginning of a hunt, when they will dash off after the dogs.

Palomino

One of the most famous horses of this century was Roy Rogers' companion Trigger. Trigger was a lovely Palomino, and when he was all decked out in his fine Western tack he was dazzling!

Palominos are named for their color, not their breeding, so a wide range of body types can be attributed to the Palomino. They are characterized by their beautifully rich, golden coats and almost pure white mane and tails. The palomino-

Origin: United States of America
Average Height: 14.1 to 17 h.h.
Aptitudes: Riding

colored horse did not originate in the United States, but it was the first country to set up a registry for this color breed. Many breeds are not capable of producing palomino coloring, such as Thoroughbreds. The so-called 'color dilution' gene must be present for palomino coloring to occur. The presence of this gene causes a lack of color, which results in the distinctive golden coat.

Royal Canadian Mounted Police Horse

One of the most well-recognized symbols of Canada has to be the Royal Canadian Mounted Police. Their famous Musical Ride tours all over the world, dazzling audiences with its great precision and style. The RCMP was established in 1873 as the North-West Mounted Police, a semi-military police force that came to stand for law, order and outstanding service in what was then the largely unsettled Canadian West. The Mounties became immigration officers, land agents, agricultural consultants, welfare officials, Indian Agents and of course police officers. In 1920 the force joined the Dominion Police of eastern Canada to become the Royal Canadian Mounted Police. Today it is possible to find Mountie memorabilia in any tourist shop in Canada.

Origin: Canada
Average Height: 16 h.h. and over
Aptitudes: Riding

The horses ridden by the RCMP, whether in the Musical Ride or for the rare street duty or crowd control, are always of the same type. They are generally of Thoroughbred extract, and occasionally Trakehner and Hanoverian stallions have been used to increase size. The mares used are usually of mixed bloodlines and have to meet a size and color standard. Always black, and standing no shorter than 16 h.h., the RCMP horse strikes a superb picture when mounted by an officer wearing the traditional red tunic and striped pants, and decked out with red appointed tack. The disposition of an RCMP horse must be very calm and gentle to deal with both the rigors of being a working police horse and the complexity of the Musical Ride. These horses are so well trained that, if their riders happen to fall, they will often finish the intricate pattern of the Musical Ride on their own. RCMP officers must serve about two or three years of active duty before they can volunteer to train for the Musical Ride. Once they become participants they will then travel to destinations all over the world to perform.

Pinto

The actual difference between a Pinto horse and a Paint horse is confusing. While most Paints can be registered as Pintos, not all Pintos can be registered as Paints. That is because Paint horses must be of a specific Paint blood line, namely Quarter Horse or Thoroughbred. On the other hand, a Pinto can be of any and all breeding, whether it is pure or crossed, as long as it meets the coloration requirement. The Pinto Horse Association of America has several categories under which a Pinto can be registered. These are according to type, such as Stock, Hunter, Pleasure and Saddle horse. The American Paint horses are generally shown in the Stock Horse category because of their breeding.

Origin: United States of America
Average Height: All sizes
Aptitudes: All apply

The same color descriptions apply to the Pinto as the American Paint: the overo pattern, which is a predominantly dark horse with white markings; and the tobiano pattern, where the horse is mostly white with dark patches. In Europe the terms 'piebald' and 'skewbald' are also used to describe Pinto markings. Piebald describes a horse with black and white coloration, and skewbald represents white and any other darker color except black. Pinto coloration can occur in many breeds, so there is no standard type of conformation.

158

Other Equines

Donkey

The exact origin of the domestic donkey is vague, but it is believed to have come from the Nubian subspecies of African Wild Ass. It was the backbone of ancient nomadic and pastoral peoples of the world, and it is still indispensable in many countries. The donkey's earliest records are from Ancient Egypt, where it was kept in large herds. From there it spread to all corners of the globe to become a beast of burden, an aid in the planting and reaping of harvests, a dairy animal and a source of food. Donkeys vary greatly depending on different uses, a testament to their long history with humans. It is possible to find feral donkeys—or burros as they are often called—in many parts of the world.

Origin: North Africa
Average Height: 10 to 13 h.h.
Aptitudes: Draft, general labor, sometimes riding

Donkeys are small and wiry, with huge ears and large wedge-shaped heads; mane dark, short and erect, with dorsal stripe continuing down back to tail; back long and withers prominent, often with a vertical bar across them; neck short, with upright shoulders; legs short and strong; hooves narrow and small; color most commonly gray-dun, with a white muzzle and eye circle, black points and dorsal stripe with shoulder bar and zebra striping on legs. Black, brown, red, white and spotted donkeys are also seen.

Mule

We have all heard the expression 'stubborn as a mule,' and the comparison is well founded. Mules are known for their extreme stubbornness, but they have also been greatly valued for their other assets. A mule is the result of a cross between a mare horse and a jack ass, and the opposite is a hinny, bred from a cross of a stallion and a jennet, a female ass. Both of these hybrid equines are sterile. Mules were first bred in the Middle East some 4000 years ago, and they have played an enormous role throughout human history. They are immensely strong, hardy and economical to feed and care for. From ancient wars, when mules were used to haul supply wagons, to the 'Wild West,' where they packed and pulled across the Plains and through the mountains, mules have indeed been essential.

Mules vary in their body type. Some tend to take more of their features from horses and some from asses, but they usually have fairly coarse looks. Often they have a characteristic dorsal stripe and cross-bar

Origin: Middle East
Average Height: Up to 16 h.h.
Aptitudes: Riding and draft

across the withers. They have large heads, with enormous ears; neck short set into prominent withers and upright shoulders; back long and hindquarters sloped and angular; legs and feet extremely strong and sound; color commonly dun, with black points and dorsal stripe, brown, black, bay and gray. Mules and donkeys are easy to identify in any field.

Oneger

The Oneger is a member of the Asiatic Wild Ass family. It lives in Mongolia, China and Iran, where it has greatly diminished in population owing to human encroachment. There are five subspecies of Oneger, and they vary slightly according to geographic region. Wild Onegers will often congregate in large herds during summer to mate and foal. Once the monsoon rains are finished, they will break into smaller groups to roam and forage.

Origin: Asia and the Middle East
Average Height: 12 h.h.
Aptitudes: Wild

Onegers resemble donkeys and burros in body shape, but they are generally larger. They have square heads, with large eyes and very long, pointed ears; neck long and slim, with a dark, very short, erect mane; shoulders upright; back straight, with broad dorsal stripe; croup sloped; legs short and wiry; hooves small and narrow; color reddish brown, with white under parts, legs, muzzle and eye-ring; eartips, mane and tail dark.

Tarpan

P eople consider the Tarpan *(Equus przewalski gmelini antonius)* to be the last link to the primitive Steppe horse, thought to be the direct ancestor to most warmbloods. The true wild Tarpan is extinct: the last wild one was killed accidentally in 1879 and the last captive one died in the Munich Zoo in 1887. Today's Tarpan is essentially a reconstructed breed. In the 19th century, the Polish government, in an attempt to re-establish the breed, selected from peasant farms horses that most closely resembled the Tarpan. These horses were usually Konick, which is the Tarpan's closest relative. Selective breeding took place to bring about a horse that was as close as possible to the original. The original Tarpan was a separate species like Przewalski's Horse, but the reconstructed Tarpan is the same species as other horses.

The Tarpan has a long head, with a straight or convex profile, smallish eyes and long ears; neck short and thick, with long, sloped shoulders and flat withers; back long and straight, with a sloped croup; chest deep; legs long and fine but very sound; color usually a dun shade, with a dorsal stripe and often a shoulder stripe; lower legs, mane, tail and ear tips dark; mane and tail often fringed with the dun coat color.

Origin: Russia and Poland
Average Height: 13 h.h.
Aptitudes: Riding and light draft

Wild Ass

Wild Asses are associated with Africa. They are considered to be the ancestor of the donkey and are the most endangered of all the equines. There is only one subspecies of Wild Ass left, known as the Somali Ass. It can be found in a few areas of Somalia and Ethiopia. Wild Asses are superbly adapted to the extreme conditions of the Somali and Ethiopian deserts. In fact, in some parts the only wild mammal to be seen is the Wild Ass! Unfortunately, human encroachment, civil unrest and habitat loss make it difficult for the Wild Ass to make a comeback.

Origin: Northern Africa
Average Height: 12.2 h.h.
Aptitudes: Wild

The Somali Ass is much like a donkey, with a large head and long ears; neck medium length with a dark, erect mane; back straight and croup sloped; legs short and wiry; feet small and narrow; color even-gray with a white belly, legs, muzzle and eye-ring; mane and tail dark, with a faint dorsal stripe and sometimes a faint shoulder bar stripe; legs covered in black zebra stripes; ears dark tipped.

Burchell's Zebra

The most common zebra species in Africa is the Burchell's Zebra. The original subspecies is extinct now, but the species is still referred to as Burchell's Zebra. There are a few subspecies, or races, of Burchell's Zebras, including Grant's and Chapman's Zebra. These small, striped equines are a breath-taking sight when seen in a large group, or when thundering away from a threat. Their striking stripes seem to be poor camouflage, but when seen from a distance in the shimmering heat of the African plains, large herds of zebra all but disappear. Their stripes actually make excellent camouflage because as a group they become indistinguishable from one another.

Quite different from asses and horses, the Burchell's Zebra—also called the Plains Zebra—has a medium-sized head, with large eyes, made to look even larger because of dark outlines; ears quite large, with black tips; neck medium length, with a stiff, short, upright mane that continues the striping of the neck; withers prominent; back straight; croup rounded and tail set low; tail tufted like a donkey's; hooves hard and narrow; striping vertical along neck and back where it curves back, becoming horizontal and forming a 'y' on the flank; stripes in general carry under the belly and are horizontal on the legs—but the true Burchell's race has almost pure white legs and no striping on the belly; shadow stripes are usually seen between the larger, darker stripes.

Origin: Africa
Average Height: 13.2 h.h.
Aptitudes: Wild

Chapman's Zebra

A zebra's stripes are like fingerprints: no two zebras will ever have the same configuration of stripes. There are often interesting examples of stripe variation: rare melanistic markings make a zebra look as though it has spots instead of stripes, and sometimes zebras look like they have white stripes on a black background rather than black on white.

Origin: Africa (north from Zululand to the Zambezi River)

Average Height: 13.2 h.h.

Aptitudes: Wild

Chapman's Zebra represents one of the different races of the Burchell's Zebra. It is found further north than the original Burchell's Zebras, has a lighter ground coat color and the stripes continue on the leg to just below the knee. Chapman's also displays the shadow stripes between the dark main stripes on the flank and hindquarters (zebras most closely resembling the original Burchell's race have no striping on the legs and under the belly as well as shadow striping between the main stripes). Chapman's Zebras are otherwise basically the same as all of the Burchell's.

166

Grant's Zebra

All of the Burchell's Zebra species live much like wild horses do, traveling in small family groups consisting of mares, juveniles and a herd stallion. Mature stallions not protecting a herd wander separately or in bachelor groups until they can acquire mares of their own to start a herd. Zebras often travel with the great herds of wildebeest. It is a symbiotic relationship where the zebras crop the long, coarse grasses of the plains, and the wildebeest follow to munch the shorter grasses left behind. The zebra's primary predator is the lion.

Grant's Zebra is the smallest race of the Burchell's species. It is found mostly in East Africa north of the Zambezi River. Grant's Zebras have striping all down the leg to the hoof and often the legs are al-

Origin: Africa (north of the Zambezi River to East Africa)
Average Height: 12.2 h.h
Aptitudes: Wild

most completely black around the fetlock, the ground color of their coat is almost pure white and they have no shadow striping. This race also has a shorter mane than the more southern races; in fact, the further north you go the less mane the zebras have. In parts of Sudan, Uganda and Somalia it is possible to see completely maneless zebras! The conformation of Grant's Zebra is generally like that of the more southern races.

Grevy's Zebra

These somewhat psychedelic-looking zebras are the largest of all the three species of zebra. Grevy's Zebras, with their long heads, gigantic ears and sometimes knock-kneed appearance, resemble mules more than the other zebras. They dwell in the semi-desert regions of northeastern Africa, in Kenya, Somalia, Ethiopia and the Sudan. They were named for a French president who was given one of these striking zebras in 1882 by the Emperor of Ethiopia.

Origin: Africa
Average Height: 15 h.h.
Aptitudes: Wild

The Grevy's Zebra is quite handsome. It has a long head with incredibly large, round ears and large, expressive eyes; neck fairly short, with a high, stiff, stand-up mane that continues the striping of neck; shoulders very upright; withers prominent; back straight, with sloped, angular hindquarters; tail set low; tail tufted with raccoon-like banding; stripes narrow and close together and almost completely vertical on the body and neck; legs fairly long and often knock-kneed, with very close, thin horizontal stripes turning into almost pure black fetlocks; hooves narrow and very tough; dorsal stripe down the back and a stripe under the belly; vertical striping extends just over halfway down the side.

Mountain Zebra

The third species of zebra, the Mountain Zebra, has two different subspecies, the Hartmann's Zebra and the Cape Mountain Zebra. Hartmann's lives east of the Namib Desert, in southern Angola and parts of South Africa. It is larger than its cousin, with smaller ears and a smaller dewlap. The dewlap is probably the most notable feature of the Mountain Zebra: it is a small, square flap of skin that hangs from the throat. Males characteristically sport larger dewlaps than females. Cape Mountain Zebras are smaller and stockier than the Hartmann's and are found primarily in the Cape Province of South Africa. Mountain Zebras are the rarest of all the zebras, and the Cape Mountain Zebra is now found almost exclusively only in reserves and parks. They do not congregate in huge herds like the Burchell's Zebras, but they do still travel in small family groups, or harems, and their call is more like a horse than an ass.

Mountain Zebras are similar to the Burchell's Zebras in their conformation, except that they have a distinctive rump pattern that is vertical instead of horizontal. They are the smallest of all the zebra species, with short heads and long,

Origin: Southern Africa
Average Height: 12 h.h.
Aptitudes: Wild

pointed ears; stripes are broad and close together on an off-white ground and do not cover the belly; body fairly long, with short legs that carry striping all the way to the small, narrow hooves, which are supremely adapted to the rocky, dry mountain terrain where it lives.

169

Przewalski's Horse

Przewalski's Horse (*Equus przewalski poliakov*), also called Asiatic Wild Horse or Mongolian Wild Horse, is the only remaining wild horse: all other horses considered to be wild are feral descendants of domestic horses. Przewalski's Horse is a separate species from the domesticated horse (*Equus calabis*), and it has 66 chromosomes to the domestic horse's 64. It is very distinct in appearance, and displays a very different social structure to other horses. Przewalski's Horses are antagonistic, constantly testing each other and vying for position within the herd. This trait is most likely the reason that these horses could never be domesticated. Other horses have a very stable social system where there is one dominant individual and all the others know their place and relationship to the herd, and so there is little conflict.

Origin: Asia, western Mongolia
Average Height: 12 to 14 h.h.
Aptitudes: Wild

Przewalski's Horse was named after the Russian explorer who came across the horses in 1881 in northwestern Mongolia, but there are actually accounts of these wild horses from centuries earlier. Attempts have been made over time to gentle these wild horses but there are only a few records of success. On the whole, they tend to become more stubborn and wild the longer they are worked with. With domestication impossible, people hunted them instead, almost to extinction. Fortunately, thanks to efforts to breed the horses in captivity, the Calgary Zoo, Botanical Garden and Prehistoric Park in Calgary, Alberta was recently able to release a small population back into its native habitat.

Przewalski's Horse is stout and extremely hardy. It has a large head, with a straight profile and very wide-set eyes; ears long and eyes smallish; neck short and deep, with a stiff, dark mane that stands erect; back longish and straight, with a dark stripe down the middle of it; croup sloped and shoulder upright; tail set low and hip short; legs short and dense, with narrow hooves; color always a primitive dun, with black points and mealy (white) markings on the muzzle and around the eyes; tail sometimes has a tufted appearance during winter; legs often have zebra stripes.

Glossary

Action: movement of the legs at all paces

Aid: any signal that a rider will give to a horse to instruct it

Barrel: rib cage area of body, from shoulder to hip

Band: refers to a group of horses

Blood stock: Thoroughbred racehorses

Bone: a measurement around the leg taken just below the knee: used to find weight-carrying ability

Break: refers to starting a young horse with initial training

Breed: a group of animals within a species that breeds true to type; most breeds are produced by humans through selective mating

Buck: a jump into the air with head down, back arched and legs stiff

Clean-legged: no feathering on lower legs

Close-coupled: deep body with short back and well-sprung ribs (opposite of slack-loined)

Coldblood: refers to any horse of draft breeding

Colt: a young, entire male horse no older than four years old

Cow-hocked: hocks that when seen from behind angle in towards each other: conformation fault

Deep through girth: vertical depth from behind wither to behind elbow

Dam: mother

Dished: concave profile of the head

Docking: amputation of the tail for appearance (not widely practiced)

Entire: a male horse that has not been gelded

Ewe-neck: top line of neck is concave as opposed to convex

Feather: long hair on lower leg around the back of the fetlock, often continuing up the leg to back of the knee

Filly: young female horse under the age of four years

Flat-ribbed: ribcage of barrel that is not rounded

Foal: baby horse under the age of one year

Forehand: front end of a horse: head, neck, forelegs, shoulder, withers

Foundation: refers to the sire or dam that was influential at the beginning of a breed

Gelding: castrated male horse or pony

Get: offspring of a stallion

Girth: circumference of a horse's body at the withers

Hand: unit of measurement given to a horse (four inches, 10 cm = one hand); height measured to top of withers (h.h. = hands high)

Herd: group of horses

Hinny: offspring of a stallion and a Jennet (female ass)

Hotblood: A horse of Oriental breeding, e.g., Arabs, Barbs and Thoroughbreds

Lope: an easy uncollected canter

Mare: female horse more than four years old

Oriental horse: a horse breed that originated in central or western Asia

Outcross: introduction of blood from another breed

Plenty of bone: refers to the density of bone in the legs (a desirable quality)

Points: muzzle, legs, mane and tail

Pony: equine that does not exceed a height of 14.2 h.h.

Roached: mane completely shaved off (hogged: mane clipped short and thinned)

Roman nosed: a definite convex profile in the head

Sickle-hocked: a weakness in conformation where the hock, when seen from the side, is bent so that the lower leg is angled too far forward

Sire: father

Sound: a horse that does not suffer from lameness in any way

Species: a group of animals that are closely related of the same genus that can interbreed viably

Splayed feet: conformation fault where feet point out, away from each other

Stallion: an entire male horse over the age of four years

Strain: a particular subdivision within a breed

Stud: a horse-breeding farm, or a breeding stallion

Tack: saddlery and harness gear

Type: term used to describe a horse that is suited for a particular activity, (e.g., Hunter, cob, show pony, racer)

Upright pastern: a conformation fault where the angle of the pastern between the hoof and the fetlock is too close to vertical

Upright shoulder: where the angle of the shoulder between the withers and the point of the shoulder is more vertical than sloped

Wall eyed: where the iris of a horse's eye is ringed with white

Warmblood: a horse with both hotblood and coldblood breeding, usually a light horse with a fine to medium frame that is suited to riding

Well let-down: desirable conformation where the hocks are close to the ground and the lower half of the leg is shorter than the upper

Well set: a term used to describe a good, smooth transition between body parts (e.g., neck is well set into sloped shoulders)

Well-sprung ribs: well-arched ribs that denote good conformation, giving a round barrel with lots of room for the heart and lungs

Index of Names